ANARCHIST STUDIES
Volume 25 Number 1

© Lawrence & Wishart 2017
Central Books Building, Freshwater Road, Chadwell Heath, RW18 1RX
www.lwbooks.co.uk
info@lwbooks.co.uk
tel 020 8597 0090

ISBN 978-1-912064-66-3

For information on submitting contributions to Anarchist Studies please visit our website
at www.lwbooks.co.uk/anarchiststudies

Subscriptions
2017 Subscription prices are (for two issues):
Personal print £20.00
Personal electronic £18.00
Institutional £140.00

Typeset by E-Type, Liverpool
Cover illustration 'Salute to Bikini', *Washington Post* (November 8, 1946).

Anarchist Studies is indexed in Alternative Press Index, British Humanities Index,
CIRA, Left Index, International Bibliography of the Social Sciences, Sociological
Abstracts and *Sonances*.

Contents

About this issue's cover: American Military Sublime

The photo of Vice Admiral H.P. 'Spike' Blandy and his wife gleefully slicing up an atomic explosion angel cake was taken on November 6, 1946.[1] Blandy had recently overseen the evacuation of one hundred and seventy six inhabitants from Bikini Atoll in the South Pacific to make way for U.S. atomic bomb testing (Bikini was part of an archipelago of islands that the U.S. took control of during the Second World War). Earlier that year, in February, Commodore Ben Wyatt had announced the plan at the close of the islanders' weekly church service, assuring his captive audience all their needs would be taken care of by the U.S. government.[2] He then likened the Bikinians to 'the Children of Israel whom the Lord saved from the enemy and led into the Promised Land'.[3]

After blasting the hell out of the atoll, the joint army-navy task force in charge of the first round of tests celebrated their achievement with a party at the Officers Club of the Army War College in Washington, D.C. The cake in the photograph was hand-crafted by bakers in Saint Louis and express shipped to Washington, just for the occasion.[4]

One of the Bikini task force's much touted scientific hands-on atom bomb 'experiments' was to leave 176 goats, 136 pigs and 3030 rats on ships moored near the test site to see what happened. The results (instant death or excruciatingly painful burns or radiation exposure), were predictable.[5] Blandy took it all in stride: 'if the ships had been manned with normal crews there would have been a great many men who wouldn't even know right after the bomb explosion that they were to die later'.[6]

His medical officer added that after fifteen days, surviving animals 'have good chances for permanent recovery' thanks to 'penicillin and blood transfusions'.[7] You can probably guess where this is going: first the goats, then the soldiers. In 1949, reports surfaced that sailors assigned to scrape paint off Bikini-irradiated ships had been hospitalized with 'enlarged hands'.[8] The navy issued a terse statement: "No

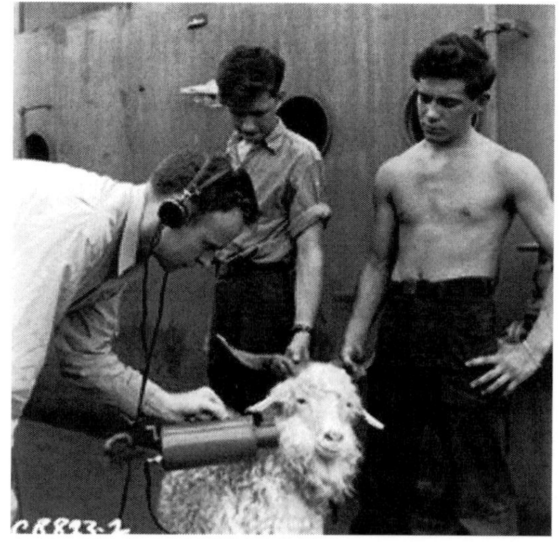

person taking part in the atomic bomb tests in the Pacific has ever been on the sick list as the result of the atomic blast'.[9]

When U.S. scientists exploded the first atomic bomb on June 16, 1945, nuclear physicist James Robert Oppenheimer, who headed the project, was so awe-struck he thought of a passage from the *Bhagavad Gita* in which the Supreme God Vishnu reveals Himself, declaring 'Now I am become Death, the destroyer of worlds'. Within two years, having reduced sublime terror to cake-like proportions, the American military was cutting into it, relishing it, and swallowing it.

Allan Antliff

NOTES

1. 'Salute to Bikini', *Washington Post* (November 8, 1946): 18 (photograph).
2. Jonathan A. Weisgall, 'The Nuclear Nomads of Bikini Island', *Chicago Daily Tribune* (Sunday, June 29, 1980): section 2, 1.
3. Ibid.
4. 'Pastor Blasts Atomic Bomb Cake Replica', *Chicago Daily Tribune* (Monday, November 11, 1946): part 1, 1.
5. Wayne Thomas, 'Find A-Bomb Killed 4rth of Bikini Beasts', *Chicago Daily Tribune* (Tuesday, July 23, 1946): part 1, 1.
6. Ibid.
7. Ibid.
8. 'Denies Navy Men Harmed in Bikini A-Bomb Blasts', *Chicago Daily Tribune* (Tuesday, October 11, 1949): part 1, 3.
9. Ibid.

Anarchist Studies 25.1 © 2017 ISSN 0967 3393

www.lwbooks.co.uk/journals/anarchiststudies/

Barnett Newman and the Anarchist Sublime

Robert B. Genter

ABSTRACT

Often overlooked in histories of abstract expressionism is the role that anarchism as a philosophy played in the art of postwar American painters like Barnett Newman. For Newman, anarchism was not merely a programme for revolutionary action but an experimental way of life that, much like painting itself, sought to imagine a life lived free from coercive authority. Through his signature painting style, which featured vertical stripes painted on coloured canvases, Newman put forth a radical political theology based on the writings of Dutch philosopher Baruch Spinoza and Russian anarchist Peter Kropotkin. In his art, Newman presented what might be called an anarchist sublime, an aesthetic experience that opened up viewers to the expressive capacity of being itself.

Keywords: *Barnett Newman, sublime, abstract expressionism, Baruch Spinoza*

In 1968, at the height of the turmoil in America surrounding the Vietnam War, Horizon Press issued a reprint of Russian anarchist Peter Kropotkin's *Memoirs of a Revolutionist*, his 1899 autobiographical account of his turn to anarchism as a revolutionary philosophy and his efforts to overthrow the Tsarist government in Russia. The Horizon edition of *Memoirs of a Revolutionist* also contained an introduction to Kropotkin's thought by activist Paul Goodman, who had spent the 1960s promoting anarchism as an alternative to Cold War liberalism and Soviet communism, and a foreword by American painter Barnett Newman, who professed the importance of Kropotkin's work to his own intellectual development. Both contrasted Kropotkin's principled stand in the late nineteenth century against 'all dogmatic systems' to the politics of the 'New Left' in the 1960s, which had, despite the movement's language, 'already begun to build a new prison with its Marcusian, Maoist, and Guevara walls'.[1] While Goodman's introduction reflected his long-time advocacy of anarchism, Newman's foreword, especially to those with only a passing familiarity with his artwork, was a surprising confession of political faith. Indeed, most art historians, even today, have failed to recognise the role that his politics played in his aesthetic project overall, despite the artist's frequent statements.[2] 'Almost fifteen years ago Harold Rosenberg challenged me to explain what one of my paintings could possibly mean to the world', Newman explained in 1962; 'My answer was that if he and others could read it properly it would mean the end of all state capitalism and totalitarianism. That answer still goes'.[3]

Regardless of such comments, historians of abstract expressionism such as Irving Sandler, Serge Guilbaut, and Michael Leja have generally ignored Newman's politics as well as those of his fellow painters Mark Rothko and Clyfford Still who professed anarchist beliefs too.[4] Instead, historians have offered two contradictory interpretations of the importance of one of the major American art movements. For decades, abstract expressionism was portrayed as a cultural rebellion of a handful of brave American artists against the staid conformity of the post-war years, artists splattering or slashing paint in trademark styles onto their canvases and heroically struggling to express their inner anguish.[5] Under this interpretation, abstract expressionism, whether in the form of Jackson Pollock's drip paintings or Willem de Kooning's chaotic abstractions, appeared as the prime example of what critic Harold Rosenberg termed 'action painting', an existential exploration of the deep recesses of the human psyche through the physical act of painting.[6] However, this conventional narrative about the heroism of the so-called New York School of painters has been challenged by claims that, despite the bravado of their language, abstract expressionists were complicit in furthering U.S. foreign policy aims during the Cold War.[7] Abstract expressionism was appropriated by politicians as a tool in the Cold War, used as one of the cultural exports sent by the U.S. government to Western Europe in the 1950s as symbols of American commitment to intellectual freedom in the face of Soviet oppression. Under this interpretation, American artists, forced to choose sides in an escalating Cold War, threw their support to the U.S. government, thereby domesticating the rebellious side of American modernism.

In many ways, these conflicting interpretations of abstract expressionism are part of a larger debate about the relationship between modernism and politics. Modernism as a cultural movement in the twentieth century was divided among those who flirted with fascism, remained committed communists, or turned to conservatism, a divide symbolised by the divergent paths of Ezra Pound, Pablo Picasso, and T.S. Eliot, for instance. Recently, however, some historians like David Weir and Allan Antliff have offered a new narrative about the history of modernism, stressing the influence of anarchist ideas in the larger cultural revolt against class divisions, sexual repression, religious orthodoxy, and other forms of oppression.[8] Emerging from the remnants of Romanticism in the nineteenth century and promoting the creative freedom of the artist, modernism upended artistic conventions by experimenting with narrative forms, collage techniques, and other radical innovations to depict the fragmented nature of modern experience in the nightmarish landscape of modernity. Much like anarchism, modernism championed a revolt against political and social norms, emerging in the early twentieth century after the repression of anarchism as a political movement in the United States, Europe and Russia. As Weir and Antliff have argued, anarchism as a political philosophy never vanished in the twentieth century, although it was eclipsed in importance by the rise of communism and fascism across Europe after World War I. Instead, anarchism found new importance within the emerging modernist culture and helped to usher in radical forms of expression in literature, painting, and poetry.

In the early twentieth century, modernist artists as varied in their interests as Francis Picabia and Marcel Duchamp were energised by the language of anarchism, which served to challenge cultural elitism and to channel revolutionary energy away from totalitarian movements into artistic innovations.[9] Often overlooked, however, was the importance of anarchism to the modernist project of those artists who came of age during the Second World War. In the midst of the horrors unleashed in Europe and elsewhere, anarchism appeared as the only alternative to the failed utopian visions that had led to such catastrophes. This was particularly true in the United States, which not only had dropped the atomic bomb but had begun an equally terrifying conflict against the Soviet Union shortly after. Countless American writers and artists, including Mark Rothko, Clyfford Still, John Cage, Allan Kaprow, Allen Ginsberg, Norman Mailer, Kenneth Rexroth, Jackson Mac Low and Donald Judd, recast post- war modernism along anarchist lines, dispensing with stale debates about Marxism and formalism and carving out an anarchist aesthetics.[10] Obviously the fissures within anarchism as a political philosophy, for instance, between the conservative, collectivist vision of P-J Proudhon and the radically individualist stance of Max Stirner, were replicated in the various forms of anarchist modernism in post-war America, but nonetheless anarchism, broadly defined as a revolt against coercive authority in all forms, flowed into American modernism. Anarchism, like modernism, spoke to the dream of a life lived outside the dictates of state or institutional control, both maintaining *la promesse de bonheur* in the face of the turmoil of the Second World War and the rise of the national security state.[11]

This was particularly true in the case of Barnett Newman who blended anarchism and modernism in his role as an 'artist-citizen'.[12] Born in New York City in 1905, Newman grew up sensitive to the political and economic inequality plaguing the United States. His father's clothing business, for instance, was forced into bankruptcy during the Great Depression, which wiped out the family's savings and forced Newman to abandon his fledgling art career for more stable employment. In the midst of such turmoil, he understood the appeal of radical movements. 'This truth, felt and understood by many intellectuals', he explained in 1933 'has driven them in what they feel to be their only possible recourse as solution and protest, to the support of the Socialist and Communist parties'.[13] Unlike many of his fellow artists, however, Newman never joined the Communist Party nor any fellow-travelling organisations during the heyday of left-wing radicalism, refusing to reduce his art to political propaganda or to ideological demands. Yet Newman did not reject radical politics in general. Instead, Newman drew inspiration from the works of Alexander Herzen and Peter Kropotkin as a challenge to the 'shouting dogmatists, Marxist, Leninist, Stalinist, and Trotskyite alike'.[14] Anarchism, as Newman explained later in life, 'is the only criticism of society which is not a technique for the seizure and transfer of power by one group against another, which is what all such doctrines amount to – the substitution of one authority for another'.[15] Newman even ran for the office of the mayor of New York City in 1933 on a campaign platform with anarchist tones, including calls for free publically funded cultural institutions. Newman also challenged chauvinistic and xenophobic politics, such as when he lambasted isolationist sentiment in the United States, which he saw as a façade for Nazi sympathy, at the start of the Second World War.

For Newman, however, anarchism was not merely a political critique or a programme for revolutionary action but a 'creative way of life' that, much like painting itself, sought to fashion more liberating forms of existence and to imagine a life lived free from coercive authority.[16] In contrast to many modernists and anarchists, however, Newman did not put forward a negative conception of freedom that promoted a radical form of autonomy outside any social grounding. Borrowing language from the Dutch philosopher Baruch Spinoza and from Russian anarchist Peter Kropotkin, Newman presented an ontology of immanence, one in which all forms of political and religious authority based on some transcendent source were levelled in favour of an image of the universe as one single substance in a constant state of flux. Through his signature painting style, which featured vertical stripes (or what he called 'zips') painted on coloured canvases, and through his frequent artistic statements, Newman put forth a radical political theology that overturned strictly mechanical or materialist conceptions of the world. Painting for Newman did not exist to represent the world but to challenge any form of representation that sought to capture the world or to present a permanent state of affairs. His art presented instead what might be called an anarchist sublime, a form of aesthetic experience that, unlike traditional understandings, tried to open up individuals to the expressive capacity of being itself. Challenging traditional notions of the sublime, which either, following Edmund Burke, reduced the experience to a feeling of powerlessness and fear, or, echoing Immanuel Kant, translated it into an intellectual experience, Newman drew upon Spinoza and Kropotkin to present the sublime instead as an empowering experience that extended the boundaries of the self while simultaneously reaffirmed the power of individual expression. In this way, Newman blended modernism and anarchism, presenting an artistic vision that had little in common with the retrograde politics of the U.S. State Department and with simplistic notions of art as merely a therapeutic practice.

FROM TRANSCENDENCE TO IMMANENCE

In 1966, the Solomon R. Guggenheim Museum in New York City, as part of their retrospective on the work of Barnett Newman, presented his recently completed series, *The Stations of the Cross: Lema Sabachthani*. Composed of fourteen paintings, each comprised of vertical stripes of white and black paint on unfinished canvases, Newman's series represented, according to him, the 'emotional complexity' of the Passion story, reflecting his long-time interest in religious themes from the Judeo-Christian tradition.[17] Born into an immigrant Jewish family in New York City, Newman received his religious education as a young boy at the National Hebrew School in the Bronx and also from his father, Abraham, whose own religious leanings were shaped by a commitment to Zionism.[18] Although he rarely spoke of his religious beliefs, Newman borrowed heavily from Talmudic, Kabbalistic, and Christian sources to explain his aesthetic project and to title his works, including for instance, *Cathedra* (1951), *Uriel* (1955), and, most obviously, his *Stations of the Cross* series. Eschewing any literal representation, Newman translated the liturgical narrative of Christ's crucifixion into a series of expressive zips –some as razor-sharp black verticals, some as faint white verticals, and some as negatively formed bands of empty canvas between two fiery painted areas. Newman's title borrowed from the Gospel of Matthew ('My God, My God, why have you forsaken me?'), thus focusing not on the entirety of the Passion story but specifically on Christ's cry of dereliction on the cross. As Newman explained, 'the cry of *Lema* – for what purpose? – this is the Passion and this is what I have tried to evoke in these paintings', and he hoped his series conveyed the spiritual pain of the event itself.[19]

In part, Newman's reference to the story of Christ wavering in his faith at the moment of his death was prompted by the anguish Newman felt in the aftermath of World War II, and much of his early artwork was an expression of a world in despair. Although Newman had a long-time interest in painting, taking courses at the Arts Student League in the 1920s and working as an art teacher in the 1930s, he only took up painting professionally toward the end of the war.[20] Borrowing themes from Native American traditions and Greek mythology, Newman, in his paintings from the mid-1940s, translated the terror of a world on the brink of annihilation into a series of canvases replete with images of the existential void at the centre of human existence, which he described as 'the hard, black chaos that is death, or the greyer, softer chaos that is tragedy'.[21] In *Pagan Void* (1946), for instance, which features a black circular void at the centre of an abstract, organic form, Newman referenced that cataclysmic power of the atomic bomb. In other early works such as *Gea* (1944-45) and *Genetic Moment* (1947), Newman presented, in Kierkegaardian terms, the 'void from which and around which life emanated', what he saw as the profound emptiness that the war had revealed.[22] But Newman quickly dropped his existential moaning, prompted in part by the fortuitous artistic advancement he made in 1948. In his studio that year he had prepared a canvas with a layer of reddish brown paint and then applied vertically a piece of adhesive tape down the centre, over which he applied thick reddish orange paint. Originally Newman had planned on removing the tape and using the background to begin a different painting, but he was struck by the effect he had serendipitously produced. According to Newman, he had started working on the canvas on his birthday and 'lived with that painting for almost a year trying to understand it'.[23] Eventually titling the painting *Onement I*, Newman recognised that he had moved beyond trying to depict some cosmic void that reflected the tragic human condition or trying to imagine some spiritual rebirth from the darkness. Instead, his new painting, with its reference to the Jewish notion of atonement, was wholeness itself, a vertical stripe that filled the surface of the canvas instead of, as he had done in his earlier paintings, emptying it. As he explained, the zip 'does not cut the format in half or in whatever parts, but it does the exact opposite: it unites the thing'.[24] From that moment, Newman radically shifted his aesthetic thinking, replacing the 'hated' void with an entirely different ontology.[25]

Instead of painting the void, he sought to paint fullness, a project that culminated with his *Stations* series. Newman had no interest in traditional readings of the Seven Words of Jesus on the Cross or in Christian liturgical practices associated with those words. His paintings 'can exist without a church', he explained.[26] Salvation was not his goal, for Newman saw a different message in the Passion story.

Newman refused to accept the convoluted logic that the death of Christ, God's only begotten son, was necessary to redeem humankind, a sacrifice that seemed perverse given the supposed omnipotence of God. Like Christ himself, whose cry marked his questioning of God's divine plan, Newman argued that the significance of Christ's sacrifice had nothing to do with delivering humankind from evil or helping humanity atone for sin. Instead, the Incarnation heralded God's descent to the realm of humanity through His son – stepping down from His throne, becoming a part of His own divine creation, and participating in the suffering of humanity. In this sense, the Incarnation marked the transition from the transcendent God-the-Father to the immanence of the Holy Spirit. According to such a reading, Christ's death ended the cycle of legal retribution for the sins of humanity by calling into question the entire system of justice established by the Abrahamic tradition. As Newman explained, 'the cry, the unanswerable cry, is world without end', that is, a world not supported by divine authority.[27] Newman refused to lapse into nihilism, however, although he was aware of the existential anguish expressed by Christ's cry of abandonment. Instead, he welcomed the end to any notion of a divine authority and sought, however overwhelming, the experience of immanence.

The *Stations* series was based not only on Newman's interpretation of the Passion story but on his reading of the works of Baruch Spinoza, the seventeenth-century Dutch philosopher whose writings represented a challenge to the religious authority of the Judeo-Christian tradition. Spinoza taught the same lesson that Christ on the cross did – that human beings were no longer subservient to any transcendent authority, religious or otherwise. Newman was introduced to the philosophy of Spinoza while an undergraduate philosophy major at the City College of New York in the 1920s, and he composed his first artistic manifesto based on Spinoza's ideas after he and his fellow classmates were denied viewing access to the paintings of the Barnes Foundation in Pennsylvania in 1926. Throughout his career, Newman borrowed themes from Spinoza's philosophy and filled his personal library with many volumes, including Spinoza's *How to Improve Your Mind*, R.H.M. Elwes's translation of Spinoza's major political works, Andrew Boyle's translation of Spinoza's *Ethics*, and Rudolf Kayser's 1946 biography, *Spinoza: Portrait of a Spiritual Hero*, as well as several shorter works by the Dutch philosopher. Newman saw Spinoza as an alternative to Hegelian and Marxist philosophies, offering a radical political theology that challenged traditional notions of God as a transcendent being, overturned all forms of dialectical and tele-ological thinking, and trumpeted a dynamic ontology of immanence.

In his posthumously published *Ethics*, Spinoza challenged any philosophy of transcendence that posited two ontologically distinct substances, one more privileged than the other. Pointing to the God of the Judeo-Christian tradition who transcends human experience or to the Platonic notion of a world of forms separate from the world of appearances, Spinoza argued against any concept of a universe with two different substances, unable to find any convincing explanation for the relationship between the two. In contrast, Spinoza posited a concept of substance monism, arguing for the existence of one substance or self-contained, self-generated being that did not require something else for its existence. Substance, seen as God or Nature, was not some transcendent power separate from the world but was immanent to the world itself, an indivisible being that expressed itself through and was implicated in everything. 'Whatever is, is in God,' argued Spinoza, 'and nothing can be or be conceived without God'.[28] No longer a transcendent being, God was found only in the expression of the universe itself, a creation that was the same as its creator. According to Spinoza, God or substance expressed itself through an infinite number of attributes that consti-tuted the essence of substance and through which substance was understood, of which thought and extension were the two attributes known to human beings. The world as such was constituted in part by thinking things and extended things and by an infinite number of other unknown attributes through which substance emerged. In this sense, thought and extension were not attributes of two different substances but were dynamic expressions of one single substance. Similarly, all particular states of attributes were modes of that attribute in the sense that specific bodies were modes of extension and individual minds were modes of thought. Substance was not the transcendent but the immanent cause of all extended or thinking things, irreducible to any particular mode.

The importance of Spinoza's ontology for Newman was this notion of God as *natura naturans* (a permanent process of self-creation and expression) as opposed to *natura naturata* (a finished creation). Spinoza rejected any anthropomorphic notion of a God who directed the world toward a specific end, challenging the founda-tion of all Abrahamic traditions. In asserting the immanent relationship between God, humanity, and the world, Spinoza freed human beings from subservience to any transcendent being. 'The Passion', as Newman explained, 'is not a protest but a declaration' of a new ontology of immanence.[29] Instead of a world subjected to endless hierarchies and divisions, Spinoza presented a world in a constant state of becoming, part of the endless expression of substance through the appearance and disappearance of the individual modes of particular attributes. Such modes, according to Spinoza, were not properties of a transcendent being but the expres-sive unfolding of substance in a particular fashion. 'God is the efficient cause', explained Spinoza, 'not only of the existence of things, but also of their essence'.[30]

Accordingly, Spinoza declared the radical equality of all modes and the attributes through which they were expressed. In so doing, Spinoza presented a dynamic ontology, one of multiplicity and unity, substance and modes, that demonstrated the vitality, not the void, at the heart of existence.

THE DARWINIAN LESSON

Newman found in Spinoza's works a philosophical basis for the anarchist ideas he had developed. In his *Ethics*, Spinoza outlined an ontology that levelled distinctions between beings and that undercut transcendent foundations for state power or other forms of authority, which paralleled Newman's own dream of 'the possibility of an open society, of an open world, not of a closed institutional world'.[31] Exhausted by the stale debates in American radical circles in the 1940s about the nature of the Soviet Union, Newman used Spinoza to chart an alternative based on anarchist ideas. The Dutch philosopher offered a challenge to the teleological visions of Marx and Hegel, which had reduced history to a predetermined path or to the dictates of some Universal Spirit. Like Spinoza, Newman tried to imagine the possibility of a society no longer founded on appeals to some metaphysical foundation outside human development, and he remained committed to a world continually unsettled by the unexpected modifications of God's attributes. As he argued, 'Hegel's 'science' of history and all his widespread spawn of historical interpretations have about as effectively delineated history [as did Greek astrology]. And if any book should have been burnt in our time, it should have been his'.[32] In order to better understand the importance of immanence, Newman buttressed his reading of Spinoza with the work of Peter Kropotkin who, in *Mutual Aid: A Factor of Evolution* (1902), turned to evolutionary science as a way to challenge the abstract logic of Hegelian philosophy. In Kropotkin, Newman found a political framework for his Spinozian philosophy.

A geographer and a zoologist, Kropotkin based his revolutionary politics on his reading of evolutionary theory. Rejecting both Jean-Baptiste Lamarck's notion of evolution as a pattern of steady advance and Thomas Huxley's vision of evolution as an agonistic, Hobbesian process, Kropotkin put forward a theory of evolution that rethought the role of both cooperation and selfishness in the development of individual species. Kropotkin argued that mutual aid was just as much a driving force of evolutionary development as competitive struggle, claiming that the traits of cooperation and support helped species to flourish. As Newman explained, Kropotkin 'used all his scientific knowledge and ability to disprove the theory of the survival of the fittest as the valid law of nature'.[33] Instead, Kropotkin followed the lead of Darwin by stressing the unpredictable, open-ended nature of the evolutionary process. In so doing, Kropotkin echoed Spinoza's contempt for meta-narratives of human development. Through the study of Darwin's theories, 'the idea of force governing the world, pre-established law, preconceived harmony, disappears to make room for the harmony that Fourier had caught a glimpse of'.[34] In so arguing, Kropotkin challenged the dominant ethos of capitalism, which posted self-interest as the foundation for historical progress. He put forth an ethical vision that dispensed with Hegelian abstractions and with references to basic immutable instincts. Instead, Kropotkin posted an ecological development to human nature and human values that he believed had centred over time on feelings of community and mutual aid. 'Humanity is not a rolling ball, nor even a marching column', he argued in Spinozian language, 'It is a whole that evolves simultaneously in the multitude of millions of which it is composed'.[35] Kropotkin offered Newman, as did Spinoza, an ontology of immanence, one in which human beings were tied neither to the sovereignty of God nor to some teleological end but to an endless process of evolutionary becoming.

Like Kropotkin, Newman had to learn what he referred to as the 'Darwinian lesson'.[36] Newman had a lifelong interest in the natural sciences, taking classes in the 1940s at the Brooklyn Botanical Garden and graduate courses in botany and ornithology at Cornell University and spending much time throughout his career reading the latest research in those fields. Newman developed an aesthetic theory based on this notion of the world in a constant state of development, and he heavily criticised other artists such as the Dutch painter Piet Mondrian for their limited visions. Mondrian had emerged in the early twentieth century as the figurehead of abstract art, reducing his pictorial language, in a manner first charted by Cubist painters, to straight lines, primary colours, and grid patterns.[37] Mondrian described his non-representational paintings as a form of neoplasticism, his term for art that had reduced painting to pure abstraction. In part, Mondrian based his aesthetics on theosophy, the nineteenth-century occult movement that, borrowing themes from Gnosticism, sought to discover the deeper spiritual reality beyond the realm of appearances. Theosophy stressed that the historical development of humanity was part of the larger evolution of the universe in both its spiritual and material dimensions that led to the overcoming of all divisions (positive and negative, masculine and feminine, et al.) and the emergence of a harmonious higher reality. Mondrian believed his art was part of this development.[38] He turned to abstraction to open up a visual experience no longer tied to representational forms, reducing his paintings to a series of vertical and horizontal lines that were interspersed with blocks of primary colours. According to Mondrian, 'Non-figurative art shows ...

that "art" is not the expression of the appearance of reality such as we see it, nor of the life which we live, but that it is the expression of the true reality and true life … indefinable but realizable in plastics'.[39] Mondrian saw his paintings as planes of equivalence, a balance between lines and colours that gave expression to the harmonious union of elements that he believed was the teleological end of the evolutionary process.

Newman followed Mondrian in turning to abstraction as an expression of a larger evolutionary development, but he chafed against the idealism inherent in Mondrian's theosophical, almost Hegelian, vision. In response to a retrospective of Mondrian's work by the Museum of Modern Art in 1945, Newman contrasted the Dutch painter's neoplasticism to his own developing style, which he referred to as *plasmic*. Although Newman had not yet developed his mature painterly approach and was still wedded to themes borrowed from surrealism, he had already rejected Mondrian's 'bad philosophy' that had reduced abstract painting to the purity of plastic elements in a failed search for spiritual transcendence.[40] Years later, Newman was even more direct, arguing that '[Mondrian's] horizontals and verticals moved in relation to, you might say, Platonic essences about the nature of the world', a 'utopian idea' that subjected human beings to a rigid narrative of development that reeked of totalitarianism.[41] Mondrian's art abandoned the natural world for a transcendent order that bore no connection to individual human desires and was therefore inherently violent. In contrast, Newman defined his plasmic style as an effort to use the abstract forms that Mondrian had developed to dig into, not transcend, the immanent 'world-mystery'.[42] Plasmic art did not utilise geometrical forms in an effort to reduce the world to universal forms but instead gave expression to the dynamic yet immanent power of substance that continually disrupted any static forms.

In a 1947 review of American artist Theodoros Stamos's one-man show at the Wakefield Gallery, Newman outlined the theory of immanence he had learned from Spinoza. Like Newman, Stamos had begun his artistic career painting abstract biomorphic images based on his interest in the natural sciences but soon turned to muted colour abstractions. For Newman, Stamos succeeded in conveying the complexity of the world because, unlike other modern artists, Stamos sought neither to transcend nature in the search for spiritual purity nor to merely worship nature by making it 'the object of romantic contemplation'.[43] Instead, Stamos had absorbed the Spinozian lesson that nature was a productive force, full of the activity of modes that were an expression of substance. '[Stamos] redefines the pastoral experience as one of participation with the inner life of the natural phenomenon', explained Newman; 'One might say that instead of going to the rock, he comes out of it'.[44] Newman too tried to paint this Spinozian vision of immanence. Prior to his artistic breakthrough in 1948, Newman had made clear his rejection of Mondrian's project. In *Euclidian Abyss* (1946-47), Newman referenced the founder of geometry and mocked his 'pure world of esoteric mathematical truth', which Newman compared to Mondrian's plastic forms.[45] Transcendence of the natural world, whether spiritual or mathematical, was in reality, according to Newman, an abyss, and he found his artistic response to this 'systematic theology' a year later with *Onement I*.[46] Newman redefined art as an expressive force, not in the sense of a representation of the world or of the artist's personality or dreams, but as a modal expression of a dynamic world. The stripe or zip of *Onement I* was such an expression, 'an organic thing that can contain feeling'.[47] The zip, according to Newman, was actualised difference, the expression of God's attribute of extension through a particular mode that emerged from the painted background of his canvas. In this sense, Newman's zip was not a metaphor or an abstract representation of a real figure. Similarly, the zip was not a gap, a line, a division, or, more pointedly, a void. Instead, the zip was a modal expression of the ceaseless folding, unfolding, and refolding of substance itself and, like all modes, possessed divine power.

Over the course of his career, Newman formed his zips in a multitude of ways. Sometimes Newman applied adhesive tape to the canvas first before he painted the surrounding field in order preserve a strip of bare canvas for the zip; others times he painted the zip directly on top of the completed background; or occasionally he painted the zip first between two pieces of tape and then applied colour to the field. Through these various methods, Newman was able to vary the style of his zips – some had sharp edges, some bled into the surrounding fields, and others wobbled down or across the canvas. Newman also frequently changed his painterly style when creating his zips, experimenting with differences in colour, texture, and sheen in order to create variations. In *Abraham* (1949), for instance, a vertical black zip running slightly offset from the centre of the canvas is distinguished from the greenish-black background by the subtle colour difference and sheen of the zip itself. In *Joshua* (1950), by contrast, the scarlet red zip running down the far left side of the canvas bleeds into the black background, its jagged edges formed not by tape but by a palette knife. Through these subtle variations, Newman ensured that the figure-ground relationship between the zip and the coloured field is never resolved, as the two or more elements of the work continue to vacillate. The zip as an extended thing remains perceptually a part of the larger field, safeguarding the wholeness of the entire abstraction instead of separating the elements.[48] In this regard, Newman saw his canvases an expression of the unity of substance and the plurality of its modes.

To invoke this sense of immanence, Newman titled his paintings with references to the Abrahamic tradition, not as a form of exegesis but as a gesture to the divine power expressed by his zips. 'I try in my titles,' he explained, 'to create a metaphor that will in some way correspond to what I think is the feeling in them and the meaning of it'.[49] Many of his titles were taken directly from the Bible (*Abraham*, *Covenant*, and *Eve*, for example), but most were infused with this Spinozian language of immanence. Examples include *Day One*, *Here I*, *Moment*, and *New II*, all of which reflected this idea of a universe in a constant state of becoming. Art for Newman was an expression of the infinite capacity of the universe to exceed any given expression, and, as a result, he continuously referenced the divine power inherent to humankind. In a 1947 essay, 'The First Man Was an Artist', Newman argued, in a moment of anthropological speculation, that the human impulse to create art existed prior to any other. He pointed to the Genesis story of Adam, which, according to Newman, provided a 'key to the human dream'.[50] In so arguing, Newman rewrote the Biblical story of the Fall of Man. For him, the Fall had been incorrectly interpreted as a tragedy when in fact the Fall was a form of salvation, which was revealed in full by Christ's cry of dereliction on the cross. Christ's death did not redeem humankind for the act that Adam had committed but instead repeated it. As Newman explained, 'Adam, by eating from the Tree of Knowledge, sought the creative life to be, like God, "a creator of world"'.[51] Through his cry of dereliction, Christ revealed the impotence of God-the-Father and gave humankind the possibility to empower themselves through participating in the immanent power of the Holy Spirit. Consequently, after he completed his *Stations* series, Newman added one more work with the simple title *Be*. His paintings, as 'an act of defiance' against any juridical authority, conveyed a political message.[52] For Newman, the anarchist revolution was already present throughout the endless folding and unfolding of substance that constituted the dynamic ontology Spinoza outlined.

THE ANARCHIST SUBLIME

Newman's zip paintings were part of the larger turn to abstraction in American art in the post-war years. The key moment that marked this transition was the 1950 protest led by Newman and other abstract artists over the exhibition, *American Painting Today 1950*, at the Metropolitan Museum of Art, which did not feature any examples of abstract expressionism. Challenging an institution that was 'hostile to advanced art', the so-called Irascibles, a group formed by Adolph Gottlieb, Mark Rothko, and other abstract artists working in New York City, penned an open letter to the Met that was published in the *New York Times* and then featured the following year in a *Life* magazine article.[53] Indeed, the Irascibles protest was part of a larger defence of abstract art. Throughout the 1950s, for instance, art critic Clement Greenberg defended its importance, arguing that the radical nature of the movement stemmed from the abandonment of any effort to portray external reality and from the subsequent reduction of painting to the relentless experimentation with the effects of paint on a canvas.[54] Modern painters, according to Greenberg, respected the flatness of the picture plane and thereby stopped reducing their medium to merely a mirror for the outside world, creating instead layered compositions of colour and form. As Greenberg explained, modern painters 'render every element, every part of the canvas equivalent', creating textured compositions woven 'into a tight mesh whose principle of formal unity is contained and recapitulated in each thread'.[55] In particular, Greenberg championed Jackson Pollock who had asserted the 'ambiguous flatness' of the painting canvas by creating 'all-over' compositions of 'enamel paint and blotches that he opened up and laced, interlaced, and unlaced'.[56] Accordingly, Pollock had pointed the way to the 'formal essence' of painting by making the aesthetic effect of his painting, through the 'relations of color, shape, and line' on his canvases, 'optical rather than pictorial'.[57] In doing so, Pollock had successfully separated painting as a visual experience from other artistic mediums.

Greenberg, moreover, saw a pointed political purpose to abstract art. He had followed the path of many American intellectuals in the 1930s, starting as a fellow traveller and then drifting to Trotskyism and finally Cold War liberalism as the crimes committed by Stalin became more apparent. Like other post-war intellectuals such as Dwight Macdonald and Lionel Trilling, Greenberg was scarred by his own intellectual journey and worried that the turmoil that had paved the way for authoritarianism in Europe and elsewhere had likewise begun to breed fanaticism in America. 'Industrialism', explained Greenberg, 'throws up problems that are as unprecedented in the cultural as in the economic and political sphere, and which demand solutions that cut to even deeper roots'.[58] Greenberg fretted about both the appeal of utopian illusions put forth by left-wing political movements and the waning psychological strength and emotional maturity of ordinary individuals in the face of such pressures. Staunchly anti-communist, Greenberg argued that the origins of mass political movements rested in the intolerable asphyxiation produced by the recent dislocations in American life, ranging from economic catastrophe to total war and other pressures. As Greenberg argued, 'advances in culture, no less than advances in science and industry, corrode the very society under whose aegis they are made possible'.[59] Group psychology had supposedly become the norm, as frightened individuals who were unable to comprehend the world around them gave themselves over, both mentally and physically, to the party apparatus. The end result was the abdication of personal responsibility and subservience to a political movement that dispensed systematic certainties and committed murderous atrocities.

In this sense, Greenberg promoted aesthetic formalism not just to safeguard art from the corrupting hands of radical movements but to fashion a psychological defence against the lure of authoritarian thinking that had supposedly plunged the world into darkness. For Greenberg, the optical experience provided by abstract art was a therapeutic one that softened the domineering ethos of the modern world. In a 1959 *Saturday Evening Post* article, 'The Case for Abstract Art,' Greenberg described the proper way to approach formalist art, which, as he explained, provided a form of aesthetic experience that preserved certain humanist values in a rationalised society. He described the experience of modern art as a form of mimesis in which the viewer mentally imitated the internal dynamics of an artwork, following visually the contours of the brushstrokes and the rhythms of the abstract forms. As a form of 'disinterested contemplation,' this optical experience bore no relationship to experience garnered from any cognitive processes.[60] Instead, the viewer abandoned himself or herself, if only for a moment, to the particularities of the painting. 'You become all attention', explained Greenberg, 'which means that you become, for the moment, selfless and in a sense entirely identified with the object of your attention'.[61] By providing a temporary moment of abandonment, the aesthetic experience served to temper the hostile tendencies of the self through the temporary weakening of the rigid cognitive faculties that structured the world in strict categories. The viewer supposedly became less aggressive and less vulnerable to the retrograde temptations of the outside world and therefore less committed to the despotic ideologies of the twentieth century.

While Newman too fretted over the rise of totalitarian movements and accepted the understanding of the aesthetic experience of modern art as a transformative one, he bristled at the conservative approach of Greenberg, which he saw as limiting the affective capacity of art to merely the optical and as smothering, rather than enhancing, the viewer's sense of self. For Newman, art was designed to elevate the impulses of the self, not to temper them. Borrowing once again from Spinoza, Newman linked the phenomenological to the cosmological, hoping to use the affective properties of art to intensify the individual's relationship to and participation in the expressive capacity of the world. In 1947, Newman penned a response to a review by Clement Greenberg of the work of Adolph Gottlieb in which the critic, despite his high regard for recent American art, worried that the more 'metaphysical' connotations of the paintings of Gottlieb, Newman, and others had taken priority over the more formal qualities. Newman argued that Greenberg had failed to recognise the decisive break that he and Gottlieb had made with European abstraction, which sought to convey 'the nature of mathematical law'.[62] In contrast to such 'established notions of plasticity,' Newman claimed his goal was 'to bring out from the nonreal, from the chaos of ecstasy something that evokes a memory of the emotion of an experienced moment of total reality'.[63] Newman searched for a vocabulary with which to describe the aesthetic experience he hoped his work evoked, and, by the time he painted *Onement I*, began to speak of the sublime nature of modern abstraction.

By invoking the concept of the sublime, Newman challenged the formalist notion of opticality. Newman, however, was not referencing traditional theories of the sublime. He did follow Edmund Burke in distinguishing between the beautiful and the sublime, the former referring to those objects of experience that produced a sense of pleasure due to their qualities of balance and delicacy and the latter referring to those objects that evoked a feeling of terror due to their vastness. Burke's understanding of the sublime was important because he was one of the first philosophers to focus less on the experienced object itself and more on the phenomenological experience of the subject. But Burke had little to say in support of the sublime experience itself, which he saw as overpowering in nature and as eliciting feelings of tension in frightened viewers. As Newman explained, Burke 'reads like a surrealist manual'.[64] But Newman also had little interest in Immanuel Kant's theory of the sublime either, which served as the foundation for formalist readings of abstract art. Like Burke, Kant focused on the subject of experience but, as per his philosophical project, shifted the focus away from the sensuous to the intellectual experience of the sublime. According to Kant, the experience of an expansive object overwhelmed the capacity of human sensibility to comprehend such magnitude, but such an experience in turn evoked the power of human reason to present an idea of the infinite in response. For Kant, then, the sublime referred to the expansive powers of the mind to move beyond phenomenological experience and to comprehend, through its super-sensible faculties, the mind's own autonomy. Kant's 'confusion' about the sublime, as Newman explained, was inherent in his philosophy overall, as Kant disconnected human freedom from any dependence on the empirical world.[65] In contrast, Newman put forward a theory of the sublime that both restored the fullness of bodily existence denied by Kant and translated affective experience into something more than the passivity imagined by Burke.

Once again, Newman relied on Spinoza in order to understand the importance of affect to art and to the human experience in general. In his *Ethics*, Spinoza argued, following the logic of substance monism, that the mind as a mode of the attribute of thought and the body as a mode of the attribute of extension were parallel expressions of substance, both following from God's nature. Thought and extension, however, were inherently separate from one another, causally independent attributes of substance that expressed the nature of the same reality in parallel fashion. As Spinoza explained, 'each attribute of a substance must be conceived through itself'.[66] Ideas of the mind as modes of thought were independent from but of the same order and connection as physical bodies as modes of extension. But the fact that there was no causal interaction between these two attributes did not mean there was no correspondence, and Spinoza pointed to human beings, who were an expression of both thought (the mind) and extension (the body), as examples of this complexity. According to this notion of parallelism, every specific idea must by necessity have as its object a corresponding material thing, and in the case of human beings, the mind must have as its object the body. As such, what constituted the individual human being was the fact that the ideas of the mind were always of what happened to the body. Accordingly, the power of thinking paralleled the power of acting, as any bodily affect was accompanied by an idea of that affect in the mind.

By establishing this parallelism between mind and body, Spinoza rejected the Cartesian notion of the human body as a machine animated by an immaterial soul and affirmed the importance of bodily experience. As he explained, the human body as an extending thing continually encountered other bodies, which impacted or modified it, leading to a corresponding change of the idea of the body in the mind. The complexity of the human body, capable of both acting on other bodies and being acted upon, accounted accordingly for the complexity of the human mind. Such bodily encounters were what Spinoza described as affects. 'By affect', he explained, 'I understand affections of the body by which the body's power of acting is increased or diminished, aided or restrained, and at the same time, the ideas of these affections'.[67] According to Spinoza, affects were either passive or active. In some situations, the human body was subject to chance encounters and overwhelming forces, which produced a state of powerlessness. Lacking any adequate knowledge of the true causes of such forces, the individual was subject to passions such as sadness and hope that left each passive. Conversely, in more agreeable and understandable encounters, the individual experienced joy that led to an increase in the power to take self-directed action. Thus, affects were either driven by external or internal causes, resulting in either states of passivity or activity. Spinoza referred to the latter state as the drive for self-preservation or *conatus*, that is, the effort to transform passions into actions by maintaining joyful encounters. 'We strive to affirm', explained Spinoza, 'concerning ourselves and what we love, whatever we imagine to affect with joy ourselves or what we love'.[68] Spinoza was not promoting some sterile form of autonomy but instead linking the capacity to act with the increased capacity to be affected in positive ways.

Spinoza encouraged human beings to dwell fully within affective experiences that restored a sense of individual power, and Newman hoped his artworks offered such an experience. Reflecting on his *Stations* series, Newman used Spinozian language to describe his own experience with his paintings. 'Just as I affect the canvas', he explained, 'so does the canvas affect me'.[69] Newman, like Spinoza, dispensed with traditional accounts of individual agency offered by liberalism that posited freedom as the possession of autonomous individuals. If the mind was only aware of the body through the ideas of changes to the body, then the capacity to know oneself was dependent upon the capacity to be affected by other bodies. Agency, in this sense, was a process through which the conative strivings of the individual were strengthened through positive affective encounters with other extended things. Affects, therefore, were not fleeting or immediate sensations but emotional responses that served to orient the affected individual toward the world in a certain way and to help or hinder any active response. As Newman explained, 'my concern is with the fullness that comes from emotion, not with its initial explosion, or its emotional fallout, or the glow of its expenditure'.[70] When such affects were positively understood and enjoyed, the result was an increase in the conative power of the individual. For Newman, as for Spinoza, the amelioration of suffering occurred not through divine intervention but through the intensification of a productive relationship with the world.

This notion became the basis for Newman's understanding of the aesthetic experience. Newman rejected notions of the picture plane as a field into which the gaze of the viewer penetrated (as was the case with traditional representational painting) or as a visual field where the viewer mimetically traced the undulations of the all-over composition (as with abstract painting). Instead, Newman saw the aesthetic experience as an encounter between the viewer and the painting as a distinct object. As he noted in relationship to the artistic breakthrough he had made with *Onement I*, 'the painting itself had a life of its own'.[71] Newman borrowed an example from Spinoza to explain this aesthetic principle. Spinoza described an active encounter as one between two human beings who experienced a general sense of agreement or openness between them that produced a feeling of joy in both, which in turn aided in their power of action. Newman argued his paintings as objects to be encountered functioned the same way. 'It's no different really, from one's feeling a relation to meeting another person', he described; 'One has a reaction to the person physically'.[72] The aesthetic experience of his paintings was designed to be an affective one in which viewers were not drawn into the canvas but instilled with the positive affects of joy and pleasure that restored their awareness of their own bodies and their own sense of self. Freedom, in this sense, was found only through encounters with others, which undermined any claim to some pure autonomy but which served nonetheless to empower the self.

To help realise such an encounter, Newman gave specific instructions to his viewers as to the proper mode of address. In his one-person show at the Betty Parsons Gallery in 1951, Newman posted instructions. 'There is a tendency to look at large pictures from a distance', he explained to visitors; 'The large pictures in this exhibition are intended to be seen from a short distance'.[73] In a famous photograph from 1958, Newman and a friend posed in front of his painting *Cathedra*, standing within several feet of the expansive work. From this position, the viewer, according to Newman, was in the proper position to encounter and to be properly affected by his work. Newman's zips served to unify his canvas and to ensure that the viewer was not visually swept away by the coloured expanses of his paintings. Instead, the zips, as a form of extension, asserted the solidity of the painting itself. In this way, Newman offered a different kind of visual experience than that proffered by Greenberg. Newman's vertical zips served to stop the viewer's gaze from merely wandering around the horizontal expanse of the canvas (in contrast to the visual experience, for example, of Pollock's web-like compositions) and instead to make his or her gaze move both longitudinally up and down the zip and latitudinally as the zip emerged from the surrounding field. As he explained, 'my painting should make one feel, I hope, full and alive in a spatial dome of 180 degrees going in all four directions'.[74] For Newman, the aesthetic experience was a dynamic one in which the viewer established an affective and empowering relationship with the painting.

Such an experience had political import for Newman as well. Like Greenberg who aligned his formalism with Cold War liberalism, Newman linked his own aesthetic vision with his politics too. Reflecting his reading of Spinoza, Newman offered a theory of the sublime as an aesthetic experience that was tied to his anarchist principles. In a 1948 essay, 'The Sublime Is Now', Newman argued that the 'sublime content' of modern art stemmed from 'our relationship to the absolute emotions', his translation of Spinoza's notion of affect.[75] For Newman, the sublime did not refer to the creative power of a transcendent God or the grandeur of a world separate from human existence. Moreover, the sublime was neither an isolating experience as Kant maintained nor a self-shattering experience in the Burkean sense. Instead, the sublime contributed to humankind's 'sense of being aware'.[76] The affective encounter of art was not a transportive or transcendent one but, if anything, an empowering one. As Newman explained, 'I hope that my painting has the impact of giving someone, as it did me, the feeling of his own totality, of his own separateness, of his own individuality, and at the same time of his connection to others, who are also separate'.[77] In this sense, the sublime experience that Newman described was closer to Spinoza's notion of intuition. Instead of encouraging the flight from bodily existence, Newman, like Spinoza, argued that affective experience helped to increase the power of the individual to act and, equally important, to recognise, as a form of intuitive knowledge, that the individual self, like all extended beings and all thinking things, was a mode of substance.[78]

Newman's sublime affirmed the two key principles of anarchist thought he had garnered from Spinoza and Kropotkin. Art, according to Newman, was not a form of confession or representation. Instead, art was a modal expression of substance that revealed the plenitude of being. Newman demonstrated this most forcefully in his 1950-51 painting *Vir Heroicus Sublimis*, an eight-by-eighteen foot canvas that features five thin vertical stripes against an expansive red field. Like his other paintings, the zips serve to anchor the viewer against the intensity of the red paint in order to prevent the viewer's gaze from being absorbed by the colour. Newman was not trying to draw the viewer visually into his canvas but to give the experience of the infinite power of expression that constituted the essence of substance and of which humankind was a part. As he explained, 'the *fullness thereof* is what I am involved in'.[79] Moreover, he was also linking, like Spinoza and Kropotkin had done, freedom to the outcome of positive affective encounters (man, sublime). Newman refused to tie liberation merely to state functioning, utopian planning, or religious doctrine. Instead, he tied it to the creativity of social forces and forms of mutual aid and affection. In this way, Newman's anarchist sublime pointed toward a form of solidarity that did not extinguish the boundaries or activity of the individual self. Over the years, the anarchist aesthetic outlined by Newman would influence the work of later American artist such as Donald Judd and Allan Kaprow who, albeit in very different ways, borrowed Newman's notion of art as an affective experience that increased the conative striving of the individual and that challenged authoritative modes of being. This history, however, one that links post-war American modernism to anarchist thought, has yet to be written.

Robert Genter teaches in the department of history at Nassau Community College in Garden City, New York. He is the author of *Late Modernism: Art, Culture, and Politics in Cold War America* and has published numerous articles on the intellectual and cultural history of modern America.

NOTES

1. Barnett Newman, 'The True Revolution Is Anarchist!', in *Barnett Newman: Selected Writings and Interviews*, John P. O'Neill (ed.), (Berkeley: University of California Press, 1990), p50, p45, hereafter, *BN:SWI*.
2. See, for instance, the essays in *Reconsidering Barnett Newman*, Melissa Ho (ed.), (Philadelphia: Philadelphia Museum of Art, 2005).
3. Newman, 'Interview with Lane Slate', in *BN:SWI*, p251.
4. See, for example, Michael Leja, *Reframing Abstract Expressionism: Subjectivity and Painting in the 1940s*, (New Haven: Yale University Press, 1993).
5. See, for instance, Meyer Schapiro, 'The Liberating Quality of Avant-Garde Art', *Art News* 56, no. 4 (Summer 1957): 36-42; and Irving Sandler, *The Triumph of American Painting: A History of Abstract Expressionism*, (New York: Praeger Publishers, 1970).
6. Harold Rosenberg, 'American Action Painters', in *The Tradition of the New*, (New York: Horizon Press, 1959).
7. See Serge Guilbaut, *How New York Stole the Idea of Modern Art: Abstract Expressionism, Freedom, and the Cold War*, Arthur Goldhammer (trans), (Chicago: The University of Chicago Press, 1983); and Frances Saunders, *The Cultural Cold War: The CIA and the World of Arts and Letters*, (New York: The New Press, 2000).
8. See David Weir, *Anarchy and Culture: The Aesthetic Politics of Modernism*, (Amherst: University of Massachusetts Press, 1997); and Allan Antliff, *Anarchist Modernism: Art, Politics, and the First American Avant-Garde*, (Chicago: University of Chicago Press, 2001).
9. See Allan Antliff, *Anarchy and Art: From the Paris Commune to the Fall of the Berlin Wall*, (Vancouver: Arsenal Pulp Press, 2007).
10. On postwar artists and anarchism, see Tyrus Miller, *Singular Examples: Artistic Politics and the Neo-Avant-Garde*, (Evanston, Ill.: Northwestern University Press, 2009).
11. I am referring to those avant-garde forms of modernism that, according to Peter Burger, sought to overcome the division between art and life that characterised the institutional forms of high modernism associated with T.S. Eliot and others. See Peter Burger, *Theory of the Avant-Garde*, (Minneapolis: University of Minnesota Press, 1984).
12. Newman, 'Open Letter to William A.M. Burden', in *BN:SWI*, p39.
13. Newman, 'On the Need for Political Action by Men of Culture', in *BN:SWI*, p8.
14. Newman, 'The True Revolution Is Anarchist!, p44.

15. Ibid, p45.

16. Ibid.

17. Newman, 'The Fourteen Stations of the Cross, 1958-1966', in *BN:SWI*, p190.

18. On Newman's background, see Thomas Hess, *Barnett Newman*, (New York: The Museum of Modern Art, 1971), pp19-29.

19. Newman, 'The Fourteen Stations of the Cross, 1958-1966', p190.

20. See Hess, p33.

21. Newman, 'The Ideographic Picture', in *BN:SWI*, p108.

22. Newman, 'Frontiers of Space', in *BN:SWI*, p249.

23. Newman, 'Interview with David Sylvester', in *BN:SWI*, p255.

24. Newman, 'Interview with Emile de Antonio', in *BN:SWI*, p306.

25. Newman, 'Frontiers of Space', p249.

26. Newman, 'The Fourteen Stations of the Cross, 1958-1966', p189.

27. Ibid, p190.

28. Benedict de Spinoza, *Ethics*, Edwin Curley (ed. and trans), (New York: Penguin Books, 1996), p10.

29. Newman, 'The Fourteen Stations of the Cross, 1958-1966', p190.

30. Spinoza, p18.

31. Newman, 'Interview with Emile de Antonio', p308.

32. Quoted in Richard Shiff, 'Newman's Time', in *Reconsidering Barnett Newman*, p161.

33. Newman, 'The True Revolution Is Anarchist!', p51.

34. Peter Kropotkin, 'Anarchism: Its Philosophy and Ideal', in *Anarchism: A Collection of Revolutionary Writings*, Roger N. Baldwin (ed.), (New York: Dover Publications, Inc., 2002), p117.

35. Ibid, p142.

36. Newman, 'The True Revolution Is Anarchist!', p51.

37. See Carel Blotkamp, *Mondrian: The Art of Destruction*, (London: Reaktion Books, Ltd., 1994).

38. Mondrian outlined his aesthetic and religious philosophy in 'Plastic Art and Pure Plastic Art', in *Plastic Art and Pure Plastic Art and Other Essays*, (San Francisco: Wittenborn Art Books, 2008).

39. Ibid, p21.

40. Barnett Newman, 'The Plasmic Image', in *BN:SWI*, p141.

41. Newman, 'Interview with David Sylvester', p256.

42. Newman, 'The Plasmic Image', p140.

43. Barnett Newman, 'Stamos', in *BN:SWI*, p109.

44. Ibid.

45. Newman, 'Plasmic Image', p141.

46. Newman, 'Interview with David Sylvester', p256.

47. Barnett Newman, 'Remarks at Artists' Sessions at Studio 35', in *BN:SWI*, p241.

48. Newman, 'Interview with Emile de Antonio', p306.

49. Newman, 'Interview with David Sylvester', p258.

50. Barnett Newman, 'The First Man Was an Artist', in *BN:SWI*, p159.

51. Ibid.

52. Ibid, p160.

53. 'Eighteen Painters Boycott Metropolitan', *New York Times*, (May 22, 1950).

54. On Greenberg's aesthetics, see Caroline Jones, *Eyesight Alone: Clement Greenberg's Modernism and the Bureaucratization of the Senses*, (Chicago: University of Chicago Press, 2008).

55. Clement Greenberg, 'The Crisis of the Easel Picture', in *Clement Greenberg: The Collected Essays and Criticism, Volume 2*, John O'Brian (ed.), (Chicago: University of Chicago Press, 1986), p224.

56. Clement Greenberg, 'American-Type Painting', in *Clement Greenberg, Volume 3* (Chicago: University of Chicago Press, 1993), p225.

57. Clement Greenberg, 'Abstract and Representational', in ibid, pp190-1.

58. Clement Greenberg, 'The Plight of Our Culture', in ibid, p144.

59. Clement Greenberg, 'Towards a Newer Laocoon', in *Clement Greenberg: The Collected Essays and Criticism, Volume 1*, John O'Brian (ed.), (Chicago: University of Chicago Press, 1986), p22.

60. Clement Greenberg, 'The Case for Abstract Art', in *Clement Greenberg: The Collected Essays and Criticism, Volume 4*, John O'Brian (ed.), (Chicago: University of Chicago Press, 1993), p75.

61. Ibid, p81.

62. Barnett Newman, 'Response to Clement Greenberg', in *BN:SWI*, p163.

63. Ibid.

64. Barnett Newman, 'The Sublime Is Now', in *BN:SWI*, p171.

65. Ibid.

66. Spinoza, p6.

67. Ibid, p70.

68. Ibid, p83.

69. Newman, 'The Fourteen Stations of the Cross, 1958-1966', p189.

70. Newman, 'Frontiers of Space', p248.

71. Newman, 'Interview with David Sylvester', p256.

72. Ibid, p259.

73. Newman, 'Brief Statement', in *BN:SWI*, p178.

74. Newman, 'Frontiers of Space', p250.

75. Newman, 'The Sublime Is Now', p173.

76. Newman, 'Interview with David Sylvester', p258.

77. Ibid.
78. On the relation between art and affective experience, see Charles Altieri, *The Particulars of Rapture: An Aesthetics of the Affects*, (Ithaca: Cornell University Press, 2003).
79. Newman, 'Frontiers of Space', p249.

Anarchist Studies 25.1 © 2017 ISSN 0967 3393

www.lwbooks.co.uk/journals/anarchiststudies/

Proudhon's Constituted Value and the Myth of Labour Notes

Iain McKay

ABSTRACT

Karl Marx's *The Poverty of Philosophy* has played a key role in associating Pierre-Joseph Proudhon with the idea of labour-time money. This article challenges this account by demonstrating that Marx not only failed to prove his assertion but that he also ignored substantial evidence against it. Proudhon's 'constituted value' is explained and linked to other key ideas in *System of Economic Contradictions* which Marx ignores.[1]

Key words: *Proudhon, Marx, labour notes, value, exploitation, mutualism, market socialism*

Pierre-Joseph Proudhon (1809-1865) was a French working class thinker who was the first person to proclaim himself an anarchist in his seminal 1840 work *What is Property?* From then until his death – and beyond, in terms of his posthumously published work *On the Political Capacity of the Working Classes* which he dictated on his deathbed – he was one of the leading socialist thinkers in France and his influence was felt across Europe and in America. However, very little of his voluminous output has been translated into English which has led many to base their understanding of his ideas on secondary sources. At the forefront is *The Poverty of Philosophy* by Karl Marx (1813-1883).[2] This was ostensibly a reply to Proudhon's two volume *System of Economic Contradictions* which had been published the previous year, 1846. The work, whose title is a parody of the subtitle of Proudhon's book, was proclaimed by the Frenchman as 'the libel of one doctor Marx' and dismissed as 'a tissue of crudities, slanders, falsifications, and plagiarism'.[3] Unfortunately, while he made marginal notes in the copy Marx sent him, Proudhon never publicly replied to the work and as Proudhon's influence waned and Marx's rose, Marx's account of his ideas have taken root – in part due to endless repetition by Marxists.

Space precludes addressing all the inventions and misrepresentations Marx inflicted on Proudhon's work[4] so it is necessary to focus on one of the key inventions of Marx, namely the notion that Proudhon advocated 'labour-notes' (also known as 'labour-time money', 'labour cheques', 'labour vouchers', or 'time-chits'). This has been repeated by numerous Marxists discussing Proudhon's ideas and has even seeped into anarchist accounts. Kropotkin, for example, in spite stating *System of Economic Contradictions* was a 'work which, of course, lost none of its considerable merit on account of Marx's malignant pamphlet' also states that Proudhon took up 'Robert Owen's system of labour cheques representing hours of labour', thought the 'values of all the commodities' should be 'measured by the amount of labour necessary to produce them' and 'all the exchanges between the producers could be carried on by means of a national bank, which would accept payment in labour cheques'.[5]

This position is so well established in the literature that, for example, Leszek Kolakowski while recognising that 'Marx's criticism was unjust and dishonest in some respects' also reiterates that Proudhon thought 'each person should receive, from the products of others' labours, the exact equivalent of what he himself produces, and this equivalence must be measured in hours of work'.[6] It is a surprise, then, to discover that Marx never quoted Proudhon on this and instead simply asserted that his 'constituted value' meant that products 'will in future be exchanged in the exact ratio of the labour time they have cost'.[7] As will be shown, Proudhon was very clear what 'constituted value' was and it was not this. Similarly, Marx asserted the equivalence of the Frenchman's ideas with those of British socialist John Francis Bray (1809-1897) when, as will also be indicated, he was an advocate of central planning, a position completely different to Proudhon's.

As well as addressing a historic wrong, this analysis of Proudhon's ideas has current relevance in the debates within the socialist movement over market socialism.[8] With the obvious failures of Soviet-style central planning, a number of writers have sought to utilise Marx to underpin attempts to develop a model of socialism based on co-operatives exchanging goods via markets.[9] An accurate account of Proudhon's ideas – especially his theory of labour exploitation – shows that such appeals to Marx are unnecessary (particularly given his opposition to all forms of markets) and that Proudhon should be acknowledged as one of the first market socialists.

PROUDHON'S *SYSTEM*

Proudhon's two volume *System of Economic Contradictions*[10] appeared in 1846 and followed in the wake of his three *Memoirs* on property (*What is Property?* in 1840,

Letter to M. Blanqui in 1841 and *Warning to Proprietors* in 1842) and *The Creation of Order in Humanity* (1843). It built upon and extended these works by repeating his critique of capitalism and what he termed community[11] as well as utilising a methodology based on a hybrid of Kant and Hegel.

The aim of the work is to understand and critique capitalism – the economic system of its title – by building a model of it, which exposes its contradictions rather than present a history of capitalism. Proudhon organised his chapters on specific aspects of capitalism (value, division of labour, machinery, etc.) into sections about a category's thesis and antithesis. Categories were used simply as a method of analysis and presentation.[12] He started with value and the contradiction between exchange value and use value, then added the division of labour, machinery, etc. to enrich the model and make it more realistic. The goal was to show that 'the misery that grips the civilised [...] has a sole cause, not the absence of work, but a defect of the organisation in labour'[13] and how all aspects of the system combine to oppress and exploit the working class:

> we have catalogued and critiqued these forms or categories of work. They are: the division of labour, machines, competition, monopoly, the State or centralisation, free trade, credit, property and community. The result of our analysis is that if work has in itself the means of creating wealth, these means, by their own antagonism, are likely to become as many new causes of misery; and as political economy is nothing other than the affirmation of this antagonism, it is consequently proven that political economy is the affirmation and organisation of pauperism. The question is [...] how we will eliminate the pauperism which results from the inherent vice of work, or, rather, of the false organization of labour, political economy.[14]

Unlike bourgeois economists, he was well aware the current system was the latest of many and, like previous ones, could and would be replaced by another: 'guided by the idea that we have formed of social science, we shall affirm, against the socialists and against the economists, not that labour *must be organised*, nor that it is *organised* but that it *is being organised* [...] in its present form, the organisation [of labour] is inadequate and transitory'. Capitalism had to be replaced because, for example, 'machinery, like the division of labour, in the present system of social economy is at once a source of wealth and a permanent and fatal cause of misery'. Proudhon recognised the class nature of modern society and sought to indicate 'the most salient episodes and the most remarkable phases of the war between labour and capital' and how 'the increase of misery in the present state of society is parallel and equal to the increase of wealth – which completely annuls the merits of political economy'. He also noted the apologetic role of bourgeois economics: 'Political economy – that is, proprietary despotism – can never be in the wrong: it must be the proletariat'.[15]

The work is primarily a critique and Proudhon was very clear that his aim was not to present an alternative as such. This means that while the *thesis* and *antithesis* are discussed in some detail, the *synthesis* (solution) is either not mentioned at all or just in passing. In terms of positive alternatives drawn from his critique, he explicitly stated that he 'will reserve this subject ['the organisation of labour'] for the time when, the theory of economic contradictions being finished, we shall have found in their general equation the programme of association, which we shall then publish in contrast with the practice and conceptions of our predecessors'.[16] While he names his alternative mutualism[17] for the first time, it is sketched for the focus is very much on analysing and understanding capitalism and its tendencies.

Proudhon's aim was social equality and he argued that the development of capitalism creates the preconditions for socialism. This explains his opposition to the utopian socialists who simply denounced capitalism while inventing ideal systems to replace it:

> It is important, then, that we should resume the study of economic facts and practices, discover their meaning, and formulate their philosophy. Until this is done, no knowledge of social progress can be acquired, no reform attempted. The error of socialism has consisted hitherto in perpetuating religious reverie by launching forward into a fantastic future instead of seizing the reality which is crushing it; as the wrong of the economists has been in regarding every accomplished fact as an injunction against any proposal for change.
>
> For my own part, such is not my conception of economic science, the true social science. Instead of offering *a priori* arguments as solutions of the formidable problems of the organisation of labour and the distribution of wealth, I shall interrogate political economy as the depository of the secret thoughts of humanity.[18]

Thus the 'guarantee of our liberty lies in the progress of our torture'.[19] Rather than abstractly compare today's grim reality to an ideal vision of tomorrow's perfect community, Proudhon analysed capitalism in order to understand it and tendencies within it which show – in embryo – what will transcend it. More: his analysis and critique of capitalism feed directly into his vision of socialism as can be seen from Proudhon's linking of his theory of exploitation to his theory of association.

Perhaps needless to say, Marx completely ignored all this. This is made easier by the shortcomings of Proudhon's two-volume work. It is full of polemics against noted individuals and on issues of the day (not all of which are economic). It is steeped in irony and sarcasm. Proudhon is at times verbose and indulges in digressions and asides from the main topic he is addressing. His analysis is scattered across many different chapters and so the reader is tasked with extracting, say, his theory of exploitation from his discussion of machinery, monopoly and property. This not only can frustrate the casual reader but it gives an unscrupulous critic immense leeway to misrepresent his ideas by quoting extensively from the first (positive) section and ignoring the second (negative) one. He sometimes expresses himself in words which, if quoted out of context, can appear to contradict his method and his theories. Even apparently redundant sections such as the prologue on God and Chapter VIII on Providence play a polemical role, the former against those French socialists who tied their politics to religion and the latter against those French economists who explained away the problems of capitalism by proclaiming that this is just the way it is and cannot be bettered. It also assumes that the reader has a firm grasp of many subjects, not least the works of economists like Adam Smith, David Ricardo and Jean-Baptiste Say.

This means that *System of Economic Contradictions* needs to be studied as a whole as key ideas are intertwined across many chapters. It is neither a book that can be superficially read nor grasped without understanding the social and intellectual context in which it was written. Nor can it be understood if the reader has 'skimmed through it in two days' and 'read the book very cursorily'[20] – as becomes clear when reading Marx's comments in his letter to Annenkov that were later expanded into *The Poverty of Philosophy*.

MARX'S *POVERTY*

Leading Trotskyist Ernest Mandel stated that *The Poverty of Philosophy* 'is the prototype of that sort of implacable polemical writing which has often inspired the pens of Marx's followers'.[21] This can only be suggested if Proudhon's work has not been read for comparing what Marx asserted Proudhon argued with his actual words shows that Marx's work is, to be polite, unreliable.

It would require a book to discuss all aspects of what is flawed about Marx's polemic. Here we concentrate on just one, Marx's attribution of labour-notes to Proudhon. This is done because, first, this part of his polemic is best known and has shaped the wider understanding of Proudhon's ideas and, second, it expresses almost everything that is wrong in Marx's reply. Showing how Marx misrepresented

Proudhon's 'constituted value' by equating it with the advocacy of labour-notes will aid in our understanding of both Proudhon's ideas and why Marx's polemic cannot be taken as a reliable work, so allowing a re-evaluation of both.

'Constituted Value'

Marx quoted Proudhon that value 'is the corner-stone of the economic structure'[22] and then asserted that his 'constituted' value 'is the corner-stone of the system of economic contradictions' and that this 'is all M. Proudhon has discovered in political economy'.[23]

Proudhon never claimed to have 'discovered' this notion – indeed, he is at pains to stress that it 'is, as we might prove easily by innumerable quotations, a common idea running through the works on political economy'[24] and repeatedly notes that 'the honour of first mention belong[s] to Adam Smith, *Remuneration is in proportion not to USE VALUES which the producer brings to the market but TO THE LABOUR INCORPORATED in these use values*'.[25] Thus we can ignore Marx's attempts to accuse Proudhon of plagiarising David Ricardo for, like Proudhon, Ricardo explicitly noted the source of his ideas lay in Smith.

So what is 'constituted value'? Marx never actually quoted Proudhon on the matter but rather asserted that in Proudhon's 'eyes the cost of production constitutes *synthetic value* or *constituted value*'.[26] Marx continued:

> Once utility is admitted, labour is the source of all value. The measure of labour is time. The relative value of products is determined by the labour time required for their production. Price is the monetary expression of the relative value of a product. Finally, the constituted value of a product is purely and simply the value which is constituted by the labour time incorporated in it.[27]

It is correct to state that Proudhon, like Smith and Ricardo, argued that the natural price of a commodity was determined by the labour required to produce it. He indeed argued that it 'is labour, labour alone, that produces all the elements of wealth' and that this 'force which combines in certain proportions the elements of wealth' is one 'which Adam Smith has glorified so eloquently, and which his successors have misconceived (making privilege its equal) – this force is LABOUR'.[28]

The issue is, as Marx suggested, 'the conclusions M. Proudhon draws from value constituted (by labour time)'. He asserted that for while the 'determination of value by labour time is, for Ricardo, the law of exchange value' for Proudhon 'it is the synthesis of use value and exchange value. Ricardo's theory of values is the scientific interpretation of actual economic life' while Proudhon's 'is the utopian interpretation of Ricardo's theory.' It is utopian because, Marx claimed, Proudhon thinks that 'marketable value [should be] determined *a priori* by labour time' resulting in 'the sale of a given product at the price of its cost of production'.[29] In short:

> Suppose for a moment that there is no more competition and consequently no longer any means to ascertain the minimum of labour necessary for the production of a commodity; what will happen? It will suffice to spend six hours' work on the production of an object, in order to have the right, according to M. Proudhon, to demand in exchange six times as much as the one who has taken only one hour to produce the same object.[30]

Marx, then, wanted his reader to believe that Proudhon's 'constituted value' is selling products at their labour time cost: 'One hour of Peter's labour exchanges for one hour of Paul's labour. That is Mr. Bray's fundamental axiom'. An alert reader would query why, to refute Proudhon, Marx referenced a British socialist and the reason is simple – Proudhon did not advocate the position Marx assigned to him. His 'constituted value' is not labour-notes. To show this, we must *not* 'reply in a few words to Mr. Bray who without us and in spite of us had managed to supplant M. Proudhon' but instead look at Proudhon's work.[31]

For Proudhon, 'if labour cannot find its reward in its own product, very far from encouraging it, it should be abandoned as soon as possible'.[32] Note that he says 'product' rather than time and recognises that goods need not be sold and labour not paid:

> Ensure that for each of us well-being results exclusively from labour, so that the measure of work becomes the exact measure of well-being, and that the product of labour is like a second and incorruptible conscience, whose testimony punishes or rewards each man's actions, according to merit or demerit.[33]

The question arises, how did Proudhon think labour's reward would be determined? Only by competition for it was 'the most energetic instrument for the constitution of value' and ensured a 'reduction of general costs' for an 'exact knowledge of value [...] can be discovered only by competition, not at all by communistic institutions or by popular decree'.[34] He explicitly opposed the idea of pronouncing *a priori* prices (and pricing by labour-time cannot be anything else):

Suppose for a moment that all producers should sell at a fixed price: there would be some who, producing at less cost and in better quality, would get much, while others would get nothing. [...] Do you wish [...] to limit production strictly to the necessary amount? That would be a violation of liberty: for, in depriving me of the power of choice, you condemn me to pay the highest price; you destroy competition, the sole guarantee of cheapness.[35]

Marx was aware of Proudhon's actual position for he took him to task for 'defending the eternal necessity of competition' when previously Marx had asserted that, in the Frenchman's system, 'there is no more competition'.[36] Marx's critique is not internally consistent and misrepresented Proudhon's clearly stated position:

Competition is necessary to the constitution of value, that is, to the very principle of distribution, and consequently to the advent of equality. As long as a product is supplied only by a single manufacturer, its real value remains a mystery, either through the producer's misrepresentation or through his neglect or inability to reduce the cost of production to its utmost limit.[37]

Proudhon had already answered Marx's rhetorical question: 'Is your hour's labour worth mine? That is a question which is decided by competition'.[38] Proudhon was very clear that 'competition between workers' was 'a necessity' and every utopia 'ever imagined [...] cannot escape this law'.[39]

Constituted value also explained how net product was 'the natural reward of the worker' for its 'legitimacy' lies in 'the processes previously in use: if the new device succeeds, there will be a surplus of values, and consequently a profit, that is, net product; if the enterprise rests on a false basis, there will be a deficit in the gross product, and in the long run failure and bankruptcy'. Thus the 'proportion of values may continually vary without ceasing on that account to be subject to a law' and so 'value will still and always be none the less accurately determined, and it will still be labour alone which will fix the degree of its importance. Thus value varies, and the law of value is unchangeable: further, if value is susceptible of variation, it is because it is governed by a law whose principle is essentially inconstant – namely, labour measured by time'.[40] For Proudhon, constituted value was inherently dynamic: 'The idea of value socially constituted [...] serves to explain [...] how, by a series of oscillations between supply and demand, the value of every product constantly seeks a level with cost and with the needs of consumption, and consequently tends to establish itself in a fixed and positive manner'.[41]

Thus Proudhon had already answered Marx comment that if he 'admits that the value of products is determined by labour time, he should equally admit that it is the fluctuating movement alone that in societies founded on individual exchanges make labour the measure of value'.[42] Rather that proclaim that goods must be priced at their labour-time cost, his constituted value explains how market price is *regulated* by cost (ultimately labour) and this was 'the centre around which useful and exchangeable value oscillate [...] the absolute, unchangeable law which regulates economic disturbances' for 'whoever says *oscillation* necessarily supposes a mean direction toward which value's centre of gravity continually tends'.[43] That Marxists latter appropriated Proudhon's term ('the law of value'[44]) to summarise Adam Smith's analysis of the oscillation of a commodity's market price around its cost of production (labour cost) is a bitter irony.[45]

The notion that Proudhon wished to introduce labour-notes marked by the time of production is an invention of Marx. Proudhon does not mention pricing in labour-time but repeatedly uses the expression '*[p]roducts are bought only with products*' and notes that '[i]n economic science, we have said after Adam Smith, the point of view from which all values are compared is labour; as for the unit of measure, that adopted in France is the FRANC'.[46] He did not, no more than Smith or Ricardo, argue that this be changed to something else:

> The declaimers spoke about money as the fabulist spoke about language: they assigned all the goods and all the evils of society to it simultaneously. [...] If this praise and this blame were true, the invention of money, most astonishing according to M. de Sismondi, happiest in my opinion, made by the economic genius, would present a contradiction in the analysis; it would have, consequently, to be rejected and replaced by a higher, more moral and truer design. But it is not so: precious metals, cash and bank paper are not by themselves causes of good nor of evil, the true cause is in the uncertainty of value, whose constitution appears to us symbolically in currency as realisation of order and of well-being, and whose irregular oscillation, in the other products, is the principle of all plunder and misery.[47]

In short, 'what we call the value of any special product is a formula which expresses, in terms of money, the proportion of this product to the general wealth – Utility is the basis of value; labour fixes the relation; the price is the expression which, barring the fluctuations that we shall have to consider, indicates this relation'. Market value, then, 'reaches its positive determination by a series of oscillations between *supply* and *demand*'.[48]

This explains why Proudhon's work does not discuss how supply is determined, something reflected in Marx's mockery:

> Everyone knows that when supply and demand are evenly balanced, the relative value of any product is accurately determined by the quantity of labour embodied in it [...] Proudhon inverts the order of things. Begin, he says, by measuring the relative value of a product by the quantity of labour embodied in it, and supply and demand will infallibly balance one another. [...] Instead of saying like everyone else: when the weather is fine, a lot of people are to be seen going out for a walk. M. Proudhon makes his people go out for a walk in order to be able to ensure them fine weather.[49]

Yet Proudhon nowhere proclaimed that once value is 'constituted' producers will supply the precise amount demanded by consumers. Indeed, he did not discuss supply at all for he was well aware how supply and price were actually formed within a market economy – by means of contracts:

> every proposition of sale or purchase is at bottom only a comparison between two values – that is, a determination, more or less accurate if you will, but nevertheless effective. [...] It will not be denied that, if two manufacturers can supply one another by an account current, and at a settled price, with quantities of their respective products, ten, a hundred, a thousand manufacturers can do the same. Now, that would be a solution of the problem of the measure of value. The price of everything would be debated upon, I allow, because debate is still our only method of fixing prices.[50]

In other words, price and quantity would be negotiated between producers and consumers and in this manner – aided by competition – prices would eventually fall to their cost price (labour plus materials) and the amount demanded supplied. This did not imply that value would be fixed *a priori* for 'value is determined in society by a series of oscillations between supply and demand'. Indeed, his criticism of the advocates of community was rooted in its denial of the liberty of the producer to determine how much they would produce, for whom, when and at what price: 'Is the producer to be free or not in his work?'[51]

Proudhon 'did not propose to eliminate the private enterprise system. Market competition was to continue to regulate the prices of commodities'.[52] As two French economists noted over a century ago:

Proudhon's idea has often been contrasted with Robert Owen's labour notes, and with the scheme prepared by Mr Bray in 1839, in a work entitled *Labour's Wrongs and Labour's Remedy* [...] Proudhon's circulating notes have nothing in common with the labour notes described by these writers. The circulating notes represent commercial goods produced for the purpose of private exchange. Prices are freely fixed by buyer and seller, and they bear no relation to the labour time, as is the case with the labour notes. The final result, doubtless, was expected to be the same. Proudhon hoped that in this way the price of goods, now that it was no longer burdened with interest on capital, would equal cost of production. This result was to be obtained indirectly.[53]

As can be seen, Proudhon did not advocate labour-notes. Like Smith and Ricardo, he recognised the difference between the natural price of a good and its market price and argued that competition was the means by which the latter approximated the former and supply approximated to demand. He did not advocate pricing goods in anything other than Francs and rather than seeking the exchange the *time* of labour he wanted the *product* of labour to be exchanged: '*Products are bought only with products*'.[54]

Marx at one point acknowledged the reality of Proudhon's position by noting that 'he can think of nothing better than to give as the equivalent of a certain quantity of labour the sum total of the products it has created, which is as good as supposing that the whole of society consists merely of workers who receive their own produce as wages'. Marx then invented the notion that Proudhon 'takes for granted the equivalence of the working days of different workers' in order to 'arrive at equal payment for the workers' and so 'takes the equality of wages as an already established fact, in order to go off on the search for the relative value of commodities'.[55]

This ignores that Proudhon recognised that work 'differs in quantity and quality with the producer' and so if 'all salaries [must] be equal to product' then income will differ between workers. So if in an ethical sense Proudhon thought that a day's labour of one worker was equal to another he did not think that this was literally the case in terms of income. A worker's salary would equal whatever their product would fetch on the market as 'work is the source of all wealth'. There would be no equality of income but rather an 'equality of distribution' based on 'equality according to the measure of work'.[56]

So, for Proudhon, what would happen if a worker tried to sell a commodity for six Francs while his competitor sells it for one Franc? He would lack buyers and so would seek to reduce his costs in order to be competitive or abandon his trade for one more favourable. His competitor would have an income equal to the amount of goods he sold at one Franc a piece minus costs.

'Constituted Value' and money

Proudhon did *not* mean by 'constituted value' what Marx asserted he did. This is also shown by Proudhon's views on money.

Proudhon started by stating that gold and silver 'were the first commodities to have their value constituted'.[57] Marx quoted this passage yet he made no attempt to reconcile it with his earlier proclamation that Proudhon thought 'the constituted value of a product is purely and simply the value which is constituted by the labour time incorporated in it'.[58] If, as Marx suggests, Proudhon's 'constituted value' were labour-notes then how does he square that with Proudhon's statement that money was the first value to be constituted? He did not because he could not – for to do so would be to suggest that Proudhon thought gold and silver were currently priced in terms of hours worked to produce them, an obvious nonsense.

Rather than a system of labour-time pricing, Proudhon's 'constitution of value' is simply the recognition that because all goods are 'a representative of labour' this meant that they 'can be exchanged for some other'. In other words, that every product can become exchangeable like money for 'the monetisation of gold and silver' was 'the consecration of the law of proportionality, the first act in the constitution of values'. The aim was to ensure that 'all products of labour must be submitted to a proportional measure which makes all of them equally exchangeable' for up to now 'this attribute of absolute exchangeability' was given just 'to a special product [i.e., gold and silver], which shall become the type and model of all others'.[59]

The discussion of money in chapter two of *System of Economic Contradiction* is short, too short to be considered a definitive account and so has to be supplemented with the chapter on credit in the second volume. There Proudhon had noted that in chapter two he had 'demonstrated how, if the value of all products were once determined and rendered highly exchangeable' then all goods would become 'acceptable, in a word, like money, in all payments'. Therefore what 'we had to repress in the precious metals is not the use, but the privilege' and so the 'means of destroying this formidable force [of gold and silver] does not lie in the destruction of the medium' but 'in generalising its principle' by ensuring that 'all the products of labour had the same exchange value as money' as money was 'the only value that bears the stamp of society, the only merchandise standard that is current in commerce'. This would lead to 'the socialisation of all values, in the continuous creation of new monetary figures'. A bank-note would be 'the equivalent to the holder having actual possession of the sum paid' and 'the price stipulated and accepted for sold goods can become currency in the form of a bill of exchange'.[60]

Proudhon also made similar remarks in his chapter on international trade, arguing for 'all values' to be 'determined and constituted like money' and for 'each good' to be 'immediately and without loss, accepted in exchange for another'. This was because '[m]oney, as we said in chapter II, is a variable value, but CONSTITUTED' and so

> these goods remain the only one acceptable in payment, the suzerain of all the others, one whose value, by a temporary but real privilege [...], is socially and regularly determined in its oscillations [...] Until, by a radical reform in the industrial organisation, all produced values have been constituted and determined like currency [...] money preserves its royalty, and it is of it alone which one can say that to accumulate wealth is to accumulate power.

In short: 'ensure that all goods are equivalent to money'[61]

Marx made no mention of Proudhon's later discussions on money in spite of their usefulness in understanding his views on constituted value. This is perhaps unsurprising as it shows that the 'constitution' of value meant making all goods potentially (backing for) money rather than, as Marx proclaimed, pricing them according to time. Indeed, Proudhon is so clear that Marx cannot help but admit as much in passing: 'To say that, of all commodities, gold and silver were the first to have their value constituted, is to say, after all that has gone before, that gold and silver were the first to attain the status of money. This is M. Proudhon's great revelation, this is the truth that none had discovered before him'.[62]

This did not stop Marx ignoring that this was obviously the case by concluding that 'for M. Proudhon [gold and silver are] the example *par excellence* of the application of value constituted ... by labour time'.[63] Needless to say, he does not quote Proudhon stating that gold and silver were currently priced ... in the hours and minutes they had taken to produce. For Proudhon, money should be backed by all commodities rather than just one (gold or silver) and Marx's notion of labour-notes is unfounded. When Proudhon actually tried to put his ideas into practice in 1849 with his 'Bank of the People' it was indeed not a matter of labour notes but rather bills of exchange. Unsurprisingly, Proudhon's actual position has been recognised by other commentators.[64]

'Constituted Value' and 'surplus of labour'

Proudhon thought that 'constituted value' proved that 'all labour must leave a surplus' which, in turn, allows us to understand his theory of exploitation. The short discussion of 'surplus of labour' in chapter two of Proudhon's book does not aim, as Marx asserted, to show that the cost of individual products falls by increased productivity. Rather it aims to show that if labour alone produced wealth then 'labour must leave a surplus for each producer' and he does so with the use of an abstraction, namely the personification of society into Prometheus. This is used to abstract from individual exchanges and so indicates that the *social* (overall) surplus is not the product of some gaining at the expense of others. As he put it elsewhere: 'in society the profits of speculation are equal to the losses'.[65]

Proudhon, however, made a minor arithmetical mistake in the process of preparing his argument which Marx milked for more than it is worth. We will skip this to focus, as Marx should have, on the fundamental point Proudhon was making – namely that labour produces a surplus product above and beyond the amount needed to keep the worker and their family alive. This does not mean, of course, that some do not gain at the expense of others – quite the reverse as Proudhon explained how the few exploit the many – but this is a question of the *distribution* (monopolisation) of the surplus produced by labour.

Prometheus is utilised by Proudhon not to ignore the social relations of capitalism but to expose them for after invoking it he notes that while, in theory, 'by the progress of collective industry, each individual day's labour yields a greater and greater product, and while, by necessary consequence, the worker, receiving the same salary, must grow ever richer, there exist in society classes which *thrive* and classes which *perish*'.[66] However, he did not explain in chapter two how this happens. Instead, his theory is constructed from an analysis of the contradictions of specific elements of capitalism (machinery, monopoly, property, etc.). As it is built incrementally as his model and critique of capitalism is created, it is necessary to draw together its elements in order to fuller understand it and how similar Marx's later theory was.

First, labour did not have a value but what it created did and so labour produces value only as *active* labour engaged in the production process:

Labour is said to have value, not as merchandise itself, but in view of the values supposed to be contained in it potentially. The value of labour is a figurative expression, an anticipation of effect from cause [...] it becomes a reality through its product. When, therefore, we say: This man's labour is worth five francs per day, it is as if we should say: The daily product of this man's labour is worth five francs.[67]

Second, capitalism is marked by private property in the means of production and this creates an institutional inequality between the working class and the owning class (landlords and capitalists). Any equality between the two 'was bound to disappear through the advantageous position of the master and the dependence of the wage-workers. In vain does the law assure to each the right of enterprise, as well as the faculty to labour alone and sell one's products directly' for 'the object of the workshop [is] to annihilate isolated labour [...] When an establishment has had the time to grow, enlarge its foundations, ballast itself with capital, and assure itself customers, what can the worker who has only his arms do against a power so superior?' Those without property, 'within whose reach competition never comes, are hirelings of the competitors' as 'competition cannot by itself become the common condition' because '[b]y the formation of the company [...] competition is an exceptional matter, a privilege'.[68]

Third, this inequality of conditions means that workers have no access to the means of production and so they 'have sold their arms and parted with their liberty' to those who own them.[69] Capitalism's defining feature was not markets or exchange (which predate it) but rather labour as a commodity:

> The period through which we are now passing — that of machinery — is distinguished by a special characteristic: WAGE-LABOUR.
> Wage-labour stems from the use of machinery – that is, [...] from the economic fiction by which capital becomes an agent of production. [...] The first, the simplest, the most powerful of machines is the *workshop* [...] The machine, or the workshop, after having degraded the worker by giving him a master, completes his degeneracy by reducing him from the rank of artisan to that of common labourer [...] Machinery plays the leading role in industry, man is secondary: all the genius displayed by labour tends to the degradation of the proletariat [...]
> With machinery and the workshop, divine right – that is, the principle of authority – makes its entrance into political economy. Capital, Mastership [...] such are, in economic language, the various names of [...] Power, Authority, Sovereignty [...] the workshop with its hierarchical organisation, and machinery [...] serv[es] exclusively the interests of the least numerous, the least industrious, and the wealthiest class.[70]

Fourth, the workers labour under the control of their bosses and so 'they have executed with their hands what the thought of the employers had conceived'.[71] Property produces despotism in production:

> Thus, property, which should make us free, makes us prisoners. What am I saying? It degrades us, by making us servants and tyrants to one another.
>
> Do you know what it is to be a wage-worker? To work under a master, watchful of his prejudices even more than of his orders; whose dignity consists above all in demanding, *sic volo, sic jubeo* [Thus I wish. Thus I command], and never explaining [...] Not to have any thought of your own, to study without ceasing the thought of others, to know no stimulus except your daily bread, and the fear of losing your job!
>
> The wage-worker is a man to whom the proprietor who hires his services gives this speech: What you have to do does not concern you at all: you do not control it, you do not answer for it. Every observation is forbidden to you; there is no profit for you to hope for except from your wage, no risk to run, no blame to fear.[72]

Fifth, the employer keeps the product of the workers' labour:

> Here, then, is the proposition which the speculator makes to those who he wishes to collaborate with: I guarantee to you [the worker] in perpetuity the distribution [*placement*] of your products, if you will accept me as purchaser or intermediary [...] the entrepreneur will have more opportunity for selling, since, producing cheaply, he can lower his price; finally his profits will be larger because of the mass of the investments.[73]

Sixth, this allows capitalists to appropriate the difference between what workers create and what they receive in wages. The 'co-operation of numerous workers' produces 'an effect of collective power' and so 'the question is to ascertain whether the amount of individual wages paid by the entrepreneur is equivalent to th[is] collective effect'. The answer is no: it goes to the boss 'gratuitously' for he 'has paid nothing for that immense power which results from the union of workers' but rather 'has paid as many times one day's wage as he has employed workers – which is not at all the same thing'. He 'allots to himself the benefit of the collective power' which 'is usurpation on his part' and so the axiom '*[e]very product is worth what it costs*' is 'violated'.[74]

Exploitation occurred in production as the employer appropriated the collective force and surplus of labour of the wage-workers embodied within the products they create for them:

> I have proven, in dealing with value, that every labour must leave a surplus; so that in supposing the consumption of the labourer to be always the same, his labour should create, on top of his subsistence, a capital always greater. Under the regime of property, the surplus of labour, essentially collective, passes entirely [...] to the proprietor: now, between that disguised appropriation and the fraudulent usurpation of a communal good, where is the difference?
> The consequence of that usurpation is that the worker, whose share of the collective product is constantly confiscated by the entrepreneur, is always on his uppers, while the capitalist is always in profit [...] political economy, that upholds and advocates that regime, is the theory of theft.[75]

So in 'this system of interlocked monopolies' the worker 'is no longer anything more than a serf' to whom 'the holder of the instruments of production seems to say [...]: You will work as long as your labour leaves me a surplus'.[76] This explains 'the reason why wealth and poverty are correlative, inseparable, not only in idea, but in fact; this is the reason why they exist concurrently [...] the wage-worker [...] finds that, though promised [...] one hundred, he has really been given but seventy-five'. This results in a system that ensures that 'the subordinated worker should lose, together with his legitimate salary [i.e., his product], even the exercise of the industry which supported him'.[77] In short: 'PROPERTY IS THEFT'.[78]

It does not take long to show the similarities to Marx's later theory of surplus-value. In *Capital* he noted that '[h]uman labour power in its fluid state, or human labour, creates value but is not in itself value. It becomes value in its coagulated state, in objective form' and that the 'two characteristic phenomena' of capitalism are that the worker 'works under the control of the capitalist to whom his labour belongs' and 'the product is the property of the capitalist and not that of the worker, its immediate producer'. The capitalist buys the labour-power of 100 men and 'can set the 100 men to work. He pays them the value of 100 independent labour-powers, but does not pay them for the combined labour power of the 100'. Thus 'property turns out to be the right, on the part of the capitalist, to appropriate the unpaid labour of others, or its product, and the impossibility, on the part of the worker, of appropriating his own product'.[79] The echoes of Proudhon's analysis are obvious.

So much, then, for the sheer audacity of Marx's comment that'[i]n labour as a commodity, which is a grim reality, [Proudhon] sees nothing but a grammatical ellipsis'.[80] To make such a claim ignores two things. First, the substantial critique of wage-labour contained in Proudhon's book which argues that under capitalism 'mechanical progress [...] would have no other effect than to [...] make the chains of serfdom heavier [...] and deepen the abyss which separates the class that commands and enjoys from the class that obeys and suffers'.[81] Second, unlike the bourgeois ex-student Marx, Proudhon had to leave school and become a wage-worker in a print company to support his family and he was an employee when he was writing *System of Economic Contradictions*. So as well as analysing wage-labour, showing how it resulted in the oppression and exploitation of workers and how they could end it, Proudhon was – unlike Marx – actually experiencing its grim reality.

Marx: From 'error' to 'great merit'

Marx later came to many of the same conclusions he pilloried Proudhon for in 1847. One was the theory of exploitation and another was the measure of value:

> All the 'equalitarian' consequences which M. Proudhon deduces from Ricardo's doctrine are based on a fundamental error. He confounds the value of commodities measured by the quantity of labour embodied in them with the value of commodities measured by 'the value of labour' [...] Adam Smith takes as the measure of value, now the time of labour needed for the production of a commodity, now the value of labour. Ricardo exposes this error by showing clearly the disparity of these two ways of measuring. M. Proudhon goes one better than Adam Smith in error by identifying the two things which the latter had merely put in juxtaposition.[82]

He continued: '[i]t is beyond doubt that M. Proudhon confuses the two measures, measure by the labour time needed for the production of a commodity and measure by the value of the labour' and quotes him: '"Any man's labour", [Proudhon] says, "can buy the value it contains"'.[83] Significantly, Marx failed to provide a page reference and this is for a very good reason. Proudhon was taunting the bourgeois economists: 'Why do not the economists, if they believe, as they appear to, that the labour of each should leave a surplus, use all their influence in spreading this truth, so simple and so luminous: Each man's labour can buy only the value which it contains, and this value is proportional to the services of all other workers?'[84]

What of the 'error' Marx claimed that Ricardo exposed in Smith? Smith *did* identify value embodied and commanded – which is part of the reason Smith concluded goods did not exchange at their labour-values under capitalism. Yet, as

Marx later argued, Smith was superior to Ricardo precisely *because* he recognised the problem:

> Here Adam Smith is examining only commodity exchange in general: the nature of exchange-value, of the division of labour and of money. The parties to the exchange still confront each other only as owners of commodities. They buy the labour of others in the form of a commodity, just as their own labour appears in the form of a commodity. The quantity of social labour which they command is therefore equal to the quantity of labour contained in the commodity with which they themselves make the purchase. But when in the following chapters he comes to the exchange between materialised labour and living labour, between capitalist and worker, and then *stresses* that the value of the commodity is now no longer determined by the quantity of labour it itself contains, but by the quantity – which is different from this – of living labour of others which it can command, i.e., buy, he is not in fact saying by this that commodities themselves no longer exchange in proportion to the labour-time they contain; but that the *increase of wealth*, the increase of the value contained in the commodity, and the extent of this increase, depends upon the greater or less quantity of living labour which the materialised labour sets in motion. And put in this way it is correct. Smith, however, remains unclear on this point.[85]

Smith's 'error' was to recognise that commodity exchange between workers is different from wage-labour and produces different results. Ricardo failed to understand the issue and, in 1847, so did Marx, as Marx later came to comprehend:

> But Ricardo has by no means thereby solved the problem which is the real cause of Adam Smith's contradiction. *Value of labour* and *quantity of labour* remain 'equivalent expressions', so long as it is a question of *materialised labour*. They cease to be equivalents as soon as *materialised labour* is exchanged for *living labour* [...] Ricardo simply answers that this is how matters are in capitalist production. Not only does he fail to solve the problem; he does not even realise its existence in Adam Smith's work.[86]

Ricardo simply made an assertion. This appeal to authority on Proudhon's 'fundamental error' which in 1847 Marx thought is so important falls, as he later explained:

[Ricardo states:] 'The *value* of labour, and the quantity of commodities which a specific quantity of labour can buy, are not identical'. Why not? '*Because* the worker's product or an equivalent of this product is not = to the worker's pay'. i.e. the identity does not exist, *because* a difference exists. 'Therefore' (because this is not the case) 'it is not the value of labour which is the measure of value, but the quantity of labour bestowed on the commodity' [...] Value of labour is not identical with wages of labour. *Because* they are different. *Therefore* they are not identical. This is a strange logic. There is basically no reason for this other than that it is *not* so in practice. But it ought to be so, according to the theory. For the exchange of values [is] determined by the labour time realised in them.[87]

Proudhon's identification of the two measures was not a sign of his economic illiteracy, as Marx smugly proclaimed in 1847 but rather showed that on this issue – like so many others – the Frenchman is more advanced in his understanding of capitalism than the German. Thus Marx moved from Ricardo exposure of Smith's 'error' to admitting:

It is Adam Smith's great merit that [...] where he passes from simple commodity exchange and its law of value to exchange between materialised and living labour, to exchange between capital and wage-labour [...] he feels some flaw has emerged. He senses that somehow [...] in the actual result the law is suspended: more labour is exchanged for less labour (from the labourer's standpoint).[88]

The explanation is that, Marx unlike Proudhon, had no theory of exploitation occurring in production at this time. Commodity production, not wage-labour, is the issue for the 'relative value, measured by labour time, is inevitably the formula of the present enslavement of the worker' and '[i]ndividual exchange corresponds also to a definite mode of production which itself corresponds to class antagonism. There is thus no individual exchange without the antagonism of classes' and 'social relations based on class antagonism' are 'not relations between individual and individual, but between worker and capitalist, between farmer and landlord, etc.' Marx equated capitalism with 'transforming all men into immediate workers exchanging equal amounts of labour' (or '[a]ll men [becoming] wage workers getting equal pay for an equal time of work'[89]) when, as he later became aware, there is a fundamental difference between 'these two diametrically opposed economic systems'.[90]

Marx, unlike Proudhon, presented no analysis of the causes of exploitation nor linked it to wage-labour and instead suggested it happens because commodities are sold. 'Neither *The Poverty of Philosophy* nor the *Communist Manifesto*, nor *Wage Labour and Capital*', Ernest Mandel admits, 'contain the idea of surplus-value'.[91] As Stanley Moore suggests, this is because, in 1847 Marx presented the 'thesis that ending exploitation involves ending exchange' for 'in the capitalist mode of production exploitation takes place through exchange'.[92] In contrast, explaining how workers are exploited by capital is a key theme of Proudhon's book for 'to unfold the system of economic contradictions is to lay the foundations of universal association; to show how the products of collective labour *come out* of society is to explain how it will be possible to make them *return* to it; to exhibit the genesis of the problems of production and distribution is to prepare the way for their solution'.[93]

Proudhon understood that wage-labour results in the exploitation of labour and his solution was to reunite workers with the means of production they use. Marx in 1847 failed to understand Proudhon's analysis just as he failed to mention Proudhon's desire to end wage-labour by means of the 'organisation of labour'.

Proudhon and 'the organisation of labour'

For Proudhon, civilisation 'aims to constitute the value of products and organise labour'.[94] Marx concentrated on just one of these, namely the constitution of value, distorting it by turning it into 'labour-notes' and ignored completely the organisation of labour in spite of it being a key aspect of Proudhon's ideas. As Vincent explains 'Proudhon suggested many times that competition and association [...] could be brought into equilibrium by properly organising labour [...] The question of the organisation of labour makes its appearance in just about every [...] chapter [of *System of Economic Contradictions*]'.[95] 'So for the law of labour, equal exchange, to be genuinely achieved', Proudhon stressed, 'all the economic contradictions have to be resolved; which means [...] that outside of association liberty of commerce is still the tyranny of force'.[96]

The 'organisation of labour' is important because it indicates what Proudhon thought should replace capitalism. Marx did not mention it explicitly and asserted that '[i]f there were anything to be condemned, it would surely be the system of M. Proudhon, who would reduce the worker [...] to the minimum wage'. He suggested that in the seventy years before 1840 Britain saw 'a surplus of 2,700 per cent productivity; that is, in 1840 it produced 27 times as much as in 1770'. While 'in the existing relations of production, the wealth of the bourgeoisie has grown' for the working class, 'it still remains a very debatable question whether their condition has improved as a result of the increase in so-called public wealth'. 'According to M. Proudhon', Marx stated, 'the following question should be raised: why was not the English worker of 1840 27 times as rich as the one of 1770?'[97]

Assuming that in 1846 net production was 100 units per worker then if productivity grew at 3.5 per cent per year in the twenty-one years that passed between the appearance of Proudhon's work and the publication of *Capital*, production would have approximately doubled and after 150 years, it would have been approximately 175 times bigger. If (minimum) wages were seventy-five units per worker in 1846, according to Marx they would have been 37.5 per cent of the total produced in 1867 and a mere 0.43 per cent in 2016.

Marx proclaimed that 'to obtain this development of productive forces and this surplus labour, there had to be classes which profited and classes which decayed'. Yet who, in 'the system of M. Proudhon', gets the surplus which both he and Marx agree is appropriated by the capitalists and landlords under capitalism? Given that in Proudhon's system 'all the members of society are supposed to be immediate workers', Marx suggested that if workers get rid of their bosses and work for themselves then they will 'reduce' themselves 'to the minimum wage, in spite of the increase of wealth' produced by rising productivity.[98] In short, *the increase in wealth, the surplus, somehow disappears*. Marx is lead to this farcical conclusion because at this stage he had no theory of exploitation and simply asserted capitalist exploitation is caused by the production of commodities rather than wage-labour.

Proudhon recognised how 'the increase of misery in the present state of society is parallel and equal to the increase of wealth – which completely annuls the merits of political economy'. However, he also recognised in a new society it would be the workers – those who create the products the capitalist class monopolise due to wage-labour – for 'all labour must leave a surplus, all salaries [must] be equal to product' and so he advocated 'a solution based upon equality – in other words, the organisation of labour, which involves the negation of political economy and the end of property'.[99]

Proudhon's analysis of wage-labour and how exploitation occurred in production feeds directly into his arguments for workers' associations and socialisation: 'By virtue of the principle of collective force, workers are the equals and associates of their leaders'.[100] Rather than 'organise' labour based on *a priori* schemes (as per Jacobin socialist Louis Blanc or the utopian socialists), Proudhon argued that labour must evolve its own organisation based on the actual needs of society. All that could be done is to specify the basic principles and so the workplace of the future would be based on free access and self-management:

a commercial society [...] should lay down as a principle the right of any stranger to become a member upon his simple request, and to straightway enjoy the rights and prerogatives of associates and even managers [...] articles of association in which the contracting parties should stipulate no contribution of capital, but, while reserving to each the express right to compete with all, should confine themselves to a reciprocal guarantee of labour and salary [...] it is evident that all the tendencies of humanity, both in its politics and in its civil laws, are towards universalisation [...] towards a complete transformation of the idea of the company as determined by our statutes [...] articles of association [...] should regulate, no longer the contribution of the associates – since each associate, according to the economic theory, is supposed to possess absolutely nothing upon his entrance into the company – but the conditions of labour and exchange, and which should allow access to all who might present themselves [...] such articles of association would contain nothing that was not rational and scientific [...] In order that association may be real, he who participates in it must do so [...] as an active factor; he must have a deliberative voice in the council [...] everything regarding him, in short, should be regulated in accordance with equality. But these conditions are precisely those of the organisation of labour.[101]

This implies that '[w]hat one looks to preserve, and that in reality one pursues under the name of property, is no longer property; it is a new form of possession, without example in the past'.[102] This would be based on the socialisation of property:

> From this proposition [that 'labour is the principle of proportionality of values'] and its corollaries, 'any product is worth what it costs' and 'products are purchased with other products', results the dogma of equality of conditions. The idea of socially constituted value, or proportionality products, serves to explain [...] how social value continuously eliminates fictitious values, in other words, how industry brings about the socialisation of capital and property.[103]

Accordingly, 'all appropriated wealth must become collective wealth, as the capital taken from society returns to society' for '[m]onopoly is inflated to world-wide proportions, but a monopoly which encompasses the world cannot remain exclusive; it must republicanise itself or be destroyed' – monopoly being defined as '[a]ny exclusive exploitation, any appropriation either of land, or of industrial capital, or a manufacturing process'. Thus we can see what mutualism – defined by Proudhon as 'the synthesis of the two ideas of property and of community'– is based on: social ownership of the means of production (i.e., free access so resulting in the abolition of wage-labour) with workers' control of production (i.e., the users of workplaces and land determining how to use them).[104] This would produce social equality (abolition of classes) and an approximate equality of income over time:

> the salary of the worker is equal to his product, consumption equal to production [...] The salary, in the collective worker, is equal to the product [...] the equality of conditions and fortunes [...] is established then, by means of freedom, between industrial corporations and groups of citizens; it is constituted finally, slowly and by infinite oscillations, between individuals. But equality must be the universal end, because each individual represents humanity, and thus man being equal to man, the product must be equal to the product between all.[105]

Proudhon proposes the abolition of wage-labour by association, not 'the determination of value by labour time' as Marx described his 'regenerating formula of the future'. Proudhon was aware that this 'determination of value' was *not* 'the scientific expression of the economic relations of present-day society' since capitalism is defined by the existence of wage-labour rather than commodity production (which pre-dates it), a point Marx finally recognised decades later. Proudhon also knew that it was Adam Smith who 'clearly and precisely demonstrated' this rather than Ricardo.[106]

Like Ricardo, Proudhon considered himself to be working in the tradition of Adam Smith and this can be best seen in Proudhon's conclusion where he quotes Smith repeatedly. His position can be drawn from this quote from *The Wealth of Nations* (Book 1, Chapter 8):

> In that original state of things, which precedes both the appropriation of land and the accumulation of stock, the whole produce of labour belongs to the labourer. He has neither landlord nor master to share with him.
> Had this state continued, the wages of labour would have augmented with all those improvements in its productive powers to which the division of labour gives occasion. All things would gradually have become cheaper. They would have been produced by a smaller quantity of labour.[107]

'The justice that Adam Smith would like to establish', Proudhon wrote, 'is impracticable in the regime of property'.[108] He wished to ensure that workers do not 'share' the product of their labour with the owning class by reuniting workers with their means of production. He would, however, keep the market and this has led some to suggest that market socialism is somehow capitalist.[109] Yet, as Marx suggested, the 'historical conditions of [capital's] existence are by no means given with the mere circulation of money and commodities. It arises only when the owner of the means of production and subsistence finds the free worker available on the market, as the seller of his own labour-power'. The 'means of production and subsistence, while they remain the property of the immediate producer, are not capital. They only become capital under circumstances in which they serve at the same time as means of exploitation of, and domination over, the worker'.[110]

That Marx in 1847 did not understand the difference between wage-labour (selling your labour) and commodity-exchange (selling the product of your labour) – a distinction that he recognised in 1867 – can be seen when he berated Proudhon for holding a position the Frenchman did not advocate:

> In measuring the value of commodities by labour, M. Proudhon vaguely glimpses the impossibility of excluding labour from this same measure, in so far as labour has a value, as labour is a commodity. He has a misgiving that it is turning the wage minimum into the natural and normal price of immediate labour, that it is accepting the existing state of society. So, to get away from this fatal consequence, he faces about and asserts that labour is not a commodity, that it cannot have value. He forgets that he himself has taken the value of labour as a measure, he forgets that his whole system rests on labour as a commodity, on labour which is bartered, bought, sold, exchanged for produce, etc., on labour, in fact, which is an immediate source of income for the worker. He forgets everything.
>
> To save his system, he consents to sacrifice its basis.[111]

Proudhon aimed to end 'labour as a commodity' as he, unlike Marx at this time, recognised the difference between selling the products of labour and selling the ability to labour. Only the latter is capitalism as Marx belatedly came to understand:

> Let us suppose the workers are themselves in possession of their respective means of production and exchange their commodities with one another. These commodities would not be products of capital [...] they [the workers] would have [...] created an equal quantity of new value, i.e., the working day added to the means of production. This would comprise their wages plus surplus-value, the surplus labour over and above their necessary requirements, though the

result of this would belong to themselves [...] they would both receive the same wages plus the same profit, which would be equal to the value expressed in the product, say, of a 10-hour working day.[112]

This admission shows the weakness of Marx's assertion that Proudhon failed to recognise that economic categories 'are as little eternal as the relations they express. They are *historical and transitory products*'.[113] Proudhon himself made that exact point by noting that 'the radical vice of political economy' was 'affirming as a definitive state a transitory condition – namely, the division of society into patricians and proletarians'.[114] Marx, then, was like the bourgeois economist who 'confounds the most disparate things, association and wage-labour, usury and partnership'.[115]

The 'organisation of labour' was the only means to end capitalism and its contradictions:

> property in the sense of monopoly is done away with, but not in the sense
> of the producer's right to use the means of production as he wishes – a right
> which is the condition of personal freedom and individual sovereignty [...] he
> [Proudhon] did not contemplate a return from mechanized industry to crafts-
> manship. He was concerned rather with what he called 'industrial democracy',
> i.e., that the workers should retain control over the means of production.
> Productive units must be the collective property of all those employed in
> them, and the whole of society would consist of a federation of producers,
> both industrial and agricultural. This, among other things, would resolve the
> contradiction inherent in machinery, which on the one hand was a triumph of
> the human spirit over matter, but on the other hand spelt unemployment, low
> wages, overproduction, and the ruin of the working class. This plan would also
> resolve the contradiction in the division of labour, which was an instrument of
> progress yet which degraded human beings into mere parts of themselves.[116]

Given that 'the possession of these various instruments of production is already a monopoly' and 'inequalities [are] created by these monopolies', this socialisation indicates, how 'the work incorporated by each producer in their product be the only thing which is paid for when they come to exchange'.[117]

John Bray and Central Planning

Proudhon's 'organisation of labour' is a form of market socialism in which producer co-operatives sell the products of their labour for francs on a market in which every good could be used as backing for money. Rather than quote Proudhon on 'labour-money', Marx turned to British socialist John Bray in whom 'we think that we have discovered [...] the key to the past, present and future works of M. Proudhon'[118] and quotes extensively from his book *Labour's Wrongs and Labour's Remedy*.

This raises an obvious question: did Bray see the future society in the same way as Proudhon? The answer is no. Bray did not advocate the same kind of socialism as Proudhon – quite the reverse for Bray, like Marx, was an advocate of central planning: 'On the surface Bray's solution [...] would seem to have laid the basis for some kind of market socialism. However, a closer reading of *Labour's Wrongs* shows that his intention was to abolish the market and replace the motive force of competition by the conscious, rational, economic planning and decision-making of central and local authorities'.[119]

Marx quoted a passage by Bray that indicated the unsuitability of his own comparison:

> By means of general and local boards of trade, and the directors attached to each individual company, the quantities of the various commodities required for consumption – the relative value of each in regard to each other – the number of hands required in various trades and descriptions of labour – and all other matters connected with production and distribution, could in a short time be as easily determined for a nation as for an individual company under the present arrangements.[120]

An 'individual company' does not allocate labour and products within it by means of the market but rather conscious allocation – planning. That Bray advocated central planning is confirmed by other passages that Marx failed to quote. Thus 'joint-stock companies are formed' and 'their transactions governed by general and local boards of trade, which would regulate production and distribution in gross' for 'all the real capital of the country [...] is possessed and controlled by society at large [...] society is, as it were, one great joint-stock company, composed of an indefinite number of smaller companies'. There would be 'a power capable of regulating and adjusting the movements of society as a whole [...] directing all efforts, in one harmonious flow, to a well-defined and proper end' and 'acting throughout upon a well-known and well-tried plan of operations' using 'statistics of every kind [which would] acquire a degree of correctness and perfection such as they can never attain to under the existing system'. The 'production and transport of all kinds of commodities would be properly regulated and adjusted [...] The affairs of society at large would be regulated and controlled by general and local boards of all kinds [...] A national bank would create the circulating medium, and issue it to the managers of the various companies in proportion to the number of members in each company, or the character of their occupation'. Production and distribution, then, would be *regulated throughout society at large* – being alternatively increased, or decreased, or turned to new channels as the exigencies of society require' and 'the members of the companies would work the same number of hours and receive the same uniform rate of wages'.[121] In short: 'Competition could have no existence in a change like this'.[122]

None of this equates to anything Proudhon argued for in *System of Economic Contradictions*. Marx, then, turned Bray (advocate of planning) into Proudhon (market socialist) and Proudhon (prices) into Bray (labour-notes) in order to attack both. Neither writer was allowed to be themselves.

Marx's 'few words' against Bray in reality simply repeat Bray's own conclusions – presumably on the assumption his reader is (as with Proudhon's work) not familiar with it nor had plans to become so. Compared to Bray, Marx's discussion on planning is woefully short and based on generalising from two individuals ('Peter and Paul') to conclude that 'if all the members of society are supposed to be immediate workers, the exchange of equal quantities of hours of labour is possible only on condition that the number of hours to be spent on material production is agreed on beforehand. But such an agreement negates individual exchange'.[123]

This fails to comprehend the difficulties involved when we move from a thought experiment involving two people producing two products to something more realistic: 'a simple problem involving 2 objectives and 2 variants will have 4 solutions. With 5 objectives and 3 variations we already have 243 solutions. With 500 objectives and 10 variants (still a very simple economic planning problem) the number of solutions is 10^{500} (i.e., a '1' followed by 500 zeros). This is much more than the number of atoms in the entire universe'.[124]

Marx's alternative, then, is far easier to imagine than to implement. It ignores the complexity of a real economy as well as committing the fallacy of composition – what is feasible for two people becomes increasingly unfeasible on a larger scale. Noel Thompson's comments on Bray's planning system are appropriate here:

Bray was aware of the need to acquire systematically the information on which to base decisions of those who managed the means of production [...] Bray suffered from an inability to see and a failure to confront the magnitude of the task. Thus, for example, the problem of managing a socialist economy was likened to that of overseeing an 'individual enterprise'; a naïve suggestion which could only have been born out of an ignorance of the complex functions which the market performed and which would therefore have to be fulfilled by the central and local boards which Bray proposed.

However, leaving aside the problem of acquiring the information upon which formed economic decisions could be based, there remained the problem of how that information, once gathered, could best be used. On what basis and by reference to what criteria would calculation proceed [...] Bray spirited away the problems he has set himself'.[125]

The same can be said of Marx. As one Marxist – apparently without the slightest trace of embarrassment – admits: 'In deciding how much of any given article to produce, the planners have to strike a balance between social need, available labour-time and the existing means of production. Although Marx recognises that demand is elastic he never doubts that his proletarian planners – whose actual planning mechanisms are never discussed – will make the right equations'.[126]

This, of course, does not mean that central planning is impossible (the Soviet Union did practice a form of it for decades) just that it will not work as efficiently as hoped nor produce the classless society desired. Given this, it is understandable that many socialists who have been seeking an alternative to central planning have – always unknowingly – repeated the ideas Proudhon raised in 1846 in terms of their critiques of capitalism and state socialism as well as in their positive visions of a post-capitalist system.

CONCLUSION

Marx seriously misrepresented many of Proudhon's ideas and so we have concentrated on just one aspect of his polemic, namely that Proudhon's 'constituted value' equals 'labour-notes'. We have shown that this is not the case and, moreover, Marx also distorts the ideas of John Bray in the process. The irony is that of the two, it was not Proudhon who advocated labour-notes but Marx (most famously in his *Critique of the Gotha Programme*). Even more ironically, many of his points against Proudhon made in 1847 are refuted by Marx's own later work which is based on a deeper understanding of the issues.

Given this, it is perhaps unsurprising that '[f]rom the point of view of its discussions of political economy', Marx's book is 'an enigmatic work. Its *apparent* contents promise much, but in substance it delivers little that was of lasting relevance in the evolution of Marx's critique of political economy [...] The titles of some sections suggest a potential scope and sophistication of critical analysis that is just not realised'.[127] Regardless of Marx's later claims,[128] *The Poverty of Philosophy* is not a work of serious scholarship but rather a hatchet job which does not bother with accuracy or honesty to discredit and mock someone Marx wished to replace in terms of influence in the socialist movement.

Marx's book – deservedly – fell into obscurity after initial publication, undoubtedly because anyone familiar with Proudhon's work would have quickly seen the flaws in it. However, as Marx's influence rose this became less obvious as few bothered to read the book he was attacking. Its endless repetition by Marxists has ensured that a myth produced in a sectarian attack has become accepted as an accurate reflection of Proudhon's ideas. As shown, while Marx asserted that Proudhon advocated 'labour notes' he mustered nothing as trivial as evidence in support.

Proudhon did not advocate pricing goods by time-units and 'constituted value' was the ability of any commodity (priced in francs) to act as the backing for money by means of mutual credit and bills of exchange. He also utilised the concept to indicate what regulates the oscillations of value on the market and explain how labour was exploited by capital. While seeking to end the latter, he did not advocate ending the former. Unlike John Bray, to whom Marx compared him, Proudhon does not invent a system of social organisation to equate supply and demand at a good's labour-time cost simply because he did not advocate replacing the market and its 'law of value'.

Sadly, by taking Marx as a disinterested and reliable critic far too many since then have contributed to 'the perpetuation of a spiteful distortion of [Proudhon's] thought' produced by Marx's 'desire to denigrate the socialist thought of his contemporaries, especially of those of whom he perceived as his strongest competitors'. This means that the 'most persistent misconceptions concerning Proudhon's thought result from the continued reverence shown Marx and, as a result, his assessment of Proudhon and "utopian socialism"'.[129]

Marx's dishonest polemic has – as surely intended – hidden from generations of radicals how Proudhon's *System of Economic Contradictions* (like his other books) is an important and interesting work which, when freed from his erroneous critiques and their legacy, has something to offer us today. This does not mean that Proudhon was completely correct. His ideas do need to be critiqued – as Joseph Déjacque (1821-1864) did during Proudhon's lifetime to draw libertarian communist conclusions – it is just that Marx's *The Poverty of Philosophy* is not that work.

Iain McKay is an independent anarchist writer and researcher. He has produced *An Anarchist FAQ, Mutual Aid: An Introduction and Evaluation* as well as editing and introducing *Property is Theft! A Pierre-Joseph Proudhon Anthology* and *Direct*

Action Against Capital: A Peter Kropotkin Anthology (all published by AK Press).
He has written for *Black Flag*, *Freedom* and *Anarcho-Syndicalist Review* as well as
anarchist websites (primarily Anarchist Writers).

NOTES

1. I would like to thank Shawn P. Wilbur and Lucien van der Walt for their comments
   and suggestions.
2. 'The Poverty of Philosophy, Answer to the *Philosophy of Poverty* by M. Proudhon',
   Marx-Engels Collected Works (*MECW*) 6, pp105-212.
3. *Correspondance* II (Paris: Lacroix, 1875), pp267-8. My translation.
4. My introduction to *Property is Theft! A Pierre-Joseph Proudhon Anthology*,
   (Edinburgh/Oakland/Baltimore: AK Press, 2011) has an appendix on both Marx
   and *The Poverty of Philosophy* while its extracts from Proudhon's *System of Economic
   Contradictions* have numerous footnotes contrasting what he argued to what Marx
   claimed he wrote.
5. *Direct Action Against Capital: A Peter Kropotkin Anthology*, (Edinburgh/Oakland/
   Baltimore: AK Press, 2014), Iain McKay (ed.), p214, p183
6. Leszek Kolakowski, *Main currents of Marxism: its rise, growth, and dissolution 1. The
   Founders*, (Oxford: Clarendon Press, 1978), p210, p207
7. *MECW* 6, p132.
8. Geoffrey Hodgson's *Economics and Utopia: why the learning economy is not the
   end of history*, (London: Routledge, 1999) provides a good introduction to the
   history of market socialism and what theories are genuine forms of it. He notes that
   Proudhon's ideas 'could be described as an early form' of market socialism', p20.
9. See, for example, David Schweickart's *Against Capitalism*, (Cambridge: Cambridge
   University Press, 1993), Theodore A. Burczak's *Socialism after Hayek* (Ann Arbor:
   University of Michigan Press, 2006) and Richard Wolff's *Democracy at work: A cure
   for capitalism* (Chicago: Haymarket Books, 2012).
10. *Système des contradictions économiques ou Philosophie de la misère* (*Système*) (Paris:
    Guillaumin, 1846). All quotations from this work used in this article are either my
    original translations or revised by me from those contained in *Property is Theft!*
11. This term (*communauté*) is often translated as 'communism' but in reality Proudhon
    was referring to the schemes of such utopian socialists as Fourier and Saint-Simon.
    These communities did not aim to abolish money nor, for that matter, end property
    income. Proudhon objected to these highly regulated systems because 'the commu-
    nity is proprietor, and proprietor not only of the goods, but of the persons and wills.'
    ('What is Property?', *Property is Theft!*, p131) A large part of *System of Economic
    Contradictions* including Chapter XII (which is entitled 'La Communauté' and

dedicated to critiquing it) is directed against those socialists who presented visions of ideal communities instead of basing their ideas on developments within current society which pointed beyond it, a position Marx later echoed.

12. Regardless of Marx's assertions, Proudhon is aware that '[i]n practice, all these things are inseparable and simultaneous; but in the theory they are distinct and consecutive; and property is no more monopoly than the machine is the division of labour, even though monopoly is almost always and almost necessarily accompanied by property, as division almost always and almost necessarily supposes the use of machines' (*Système* II, pp250-1).

13. *Système* II, p418.

14. Ibid, pp419-20.

15. *Système* I, p14, p167, pp91-2, p31, p148.

16. Ibid, p176.

17. Proudhon did not invent the term 'mutualism'. The workers' organisations in Lyon, where he stayed in 1843, used it in the 1830s and 1840s and there is 'close similarity between the associational ideal of Proudhon [...] and the program of the Lyon Mutualists', (Steven K. Vincent, *Pierre-Joseph Proudhon and the Rise of French Republican Socialism*, [Oxford: Oxford University Press, 1984], p164).

18. *Système* I, p89.

19. Ibid, p178.

20. *MECW* 38, p95.

21. Ernest Mandel, *The formation of the economic thought of Karl Marx: 1843 to 'Capital'*, (London: N.L.B., 1971), p53.

22. *Système* I, p32.

23. *MECW* 6, p120.

24. *Système* I, p52.

25. *Système* II, p84.

26. *MECW* 6, p119.

27. Ibid, p120.

28. *Système* I, p55.

29. *MECW* 6, p124, p132.

30. Ibid, p136.

31. Ibid, p142.

32. *Système* I, p199.

33. *Système* II, p383.

34. *Système* I, p235, p189.

35. Ibid, pp40-1.

36. *MECW* 6, p191, p136.

37. *Système* I, p188.

38. *MECW* 6, p126.

39. *Système* I, p189. Space precludes discussing Proudhon's position on competition beyond noting he was against its laissez-faire capitalist form: 'Thus it is that, competition being one of the periods in the constitution of value, one of the elements of the social synthesis, it is true to say at the same time that it is indestructible in its principle, and that nevertheless in its present form it should be abolished, denied'. *Système* I, p205).

40. *Système* I, pp252-3, p51, p60.

41. Ibid, p87.

42. *MECW* 6, p135.

43. *Système* I, p62, p23.

44. Ibid, p60.

45. In his 1853 work *Philosophie du Progrès*, Proudhon usefully summarised both the law of value and its relationship to actual economic transitions as well as his ideas on economic reform (*Oeuvres Complètes de P-J Proudhon*, [Bruxelles: Lacroix, 1868] 20, pp91-92, pp48-56).

46. *Système* I, p246, pp67-8.

47. *Système* II, p382.

48. *Système* I, p62, p90.

49. *MECW* 6, p131.

50. *Système* I, p48.

51. *Système* II, p209, p369.

52. Dudley Dillard, 'Keynes and Proudhon', *The Journal of Economic History* 2, 1 (May, 1942): 65.

53. Charles Gide and Charles Rist, *A History of Economic Doctrines from the time of the physiocrats to the present day*, (London: Harrap, 1948), pp322-3.

54. *Système* II, p84.

55. *MECW* 6, pp129.

56. *Système* I, p55, p305, p85.

57. Ibid, p69.

58. *MECW* 6, p144, p120.

59. *Système* I, pp68-73.

60. *Système* II, pp109-111, p141.

61. Ibid, p27, p32, pp50-1.

62. *MECW* 6, p146.

63. Ibid, p151. Ironically, Marx in part bases his case on Ricardo but he later dismisses 'Ricardo's erroneous theory of money', *Theories of Surplus Value* II [London: Lawrence & Wishart, 1969], p164.

64. Dillard, p65; Jack Hayward, *After the French Revolution: Six Critics of Democracy and*

Nationalism, (Hemel Hempstead: Harvester Wheatsheaf, 1991), p189; Herbert L. Osgood, 'Scientific Anarchism', *Political Science Quarterly*, 4, 1 (March, 1889): 14-6; Charles A Dana, *Proudhon and His 'Bank Of The People'*, (Chicago: Charles H. Kerr, 1984), pp43-5.

65. *Système* I, pp77-9, p50.

66. Ibid, p80.

67. Ibid, p61. 'Marx made some disparaging remarks about this passage [...] even though Proudhon here anticipated an idea that Marx was to develop as one of the key elements in the concept of *labour power*, viz. that *as a commodity*, labour produces nothing and it exists independently of and prior to the exercise of its potential to produce value as *active* labour', Alan Oakley, *Marx's Critique of Political Economy: intellectual sources and evolution, 1844 to 1860*, (London: Routledge & Kegan Paul, 1984) 1, p118.

68. *Système* I, pp163-4, p213.

69. Ibid, p267.

70. Ibid, pp161-6. It must be stressed, contrary to the impression given by Marx, that Proudhon was *not* opposed to large-scale production: 'M. de Sismondi, like all men of patriarchal ideas, would like the division of labour, with machinery and manufactures, to be abandoned, and each family to return to the system of primitive indivision – that is, to *each one by himself, each one for himself*, in the most literal meaning of the words. That would be to retrograde; it is impossible', (*Système* I, p167).

71. *Système* I, p267.

72. *Système* II, p295.

73. *Système* I, p162.

74. Ibid, p266. Proudhon here directly references his analysis of collective force in *What is Property?*, (*Property is Theft!*, 1, pp14-7).

75. *Système* II, p315.

76. Ibid, p54.

77. *Système* I, pp258-9, p366.

78. *Système* II, p234.

79. *Capital* I, p142, pp291-2, p451, p730.

80. *MECW* 6, p129.

81. *Système*, I, p170.

82. *MECW* 6, pp127-8.

83. Ibid, p128.

84. *Système* I, p81.

85. *Theories of Surplus Value*, I (London: Lawrence & Wishart, 1969), p77.

86. *Theories of Surplus Value*, II, pp396-7.

87. *The Grundrisse*, p561.

88. *Theories of Surplus Value*, I, p87.

89. *MECW* 6, p125, p144, p138, p159, p124.

90. *Capital*, I, p931.

91. Mandel, p81.

92. Stanley Moore, *Marx versus Markets*, (University Park, Pa: Pennsylvania State University Press, 1993), p31.

93. *Système* I, p92.

94. *Système* II, p204.

95. Vincent, pp154-5.

96. *Système* II, p42.

97. *MECW* 6, pp159-60.

98. Ibid, p159, p143, pp159-60.

99. *Système* I, p31, p305, p217.

100. Ibid, p377.

101. Ibid, pp272-8. See Vincent's excellent discussion, pp154-6.

102. *Système* II, p309.

103. *Système* I, pp87-8. Space precludes discussing this aspect of Proudhon's ideas beyond noting that his support for association and socialisation is often denied (Gide and Rist, p305, p307). For a rebuttal of such denials, see my introduction to *Property is Theft!* and my critique of Derek Ryan Strong's article 'Proudhon and the Labour Theory of Property', *Anarchist Studies* 22: 1, pp52-65, 'Proudhon, Property and Possession', *Anarcho-Syndicalist Review* 66: 26-9.

104. *Système* II, p168, p528, p12, p528.

105. Ibid, pp370-1.

106. *MECW* 6, p138.

107. *Système* II, p522.

108. Ibid, p525.

109. For example, David McNally *Against the Market: Political Economy, Market Socialism and the Marxist Critique*, (London: Verso, 1993). For a critique of this position, see Justin Schwartz's review, *The American Political Science Review*, 88: 4 [1994].

110. *Capital* I, p264, p933.

111. *MECW* 6, p130.

112. *Capital* III, p276.

113. *MECW* 6, p166.

114. *Système* I, p26.

115. *Système* II, p46.

116. Kolakowski, pp207-8.

117. *Système* II, p65.

118. *MECW* 6, p138.

119. Noel W. Thompson, *The market and its critics: socialist political economy in nineteenth century Britain,* (London: Routledge, 1988), p110.

120. J.F. Bray, *Labour's Wrongs and Labour's Remedy*, (Leeds: David Green, 1839), p162.

121. Ibid, p160, p170, p194, p169, p162, p180, p181, p160.

122. Ibid, p158.

123. *MECW* 6, pp142-3.

124. Geoff Hodgson, *The Democratic Economy: A new look at planning, markets and power*, (Harmondsworth: Penguin books, 1984), pp170-1.

125. Thompson, p111.

126. Bertell Ollman, *Social and Sexual Revolution: Essays on Marx and Reich*, (Montreal: Black Rose Books, 1978), p63.

127. Oakley, pp109-10.

128. *A Contribution to the Critique of Political Economy*, (London: Lawrence & Wishart, 1970), p22.

129. Vincent, p230.

Anarchist Studies 25.1 © 2017 ISSN 0967 3393

www.lwbooks.co.uk/journals/anarchiststudies/

Alternatives to Representative Democracy and Capitalist Market Organisation: The Wintukua, Guardians of the Earth

Bernd Reiter

Nosotros nos llamamos Wintukua.
Arhuacos es el nombre que nos pusieron los colonizadores

ABSTRACT:

This essay presents the findings from field research conducted among the Wintukua, or Arhuaco, people of Colombia, in 2014. The aim of the analysis is to describe Wintukua politics, as this group practices direct, deliberative democracy. The Wintukua have some 50,000 members and live in a reservation, which they share with other indigenous groups, the Wiwa, Kaggaba (Kogi) and Kankuamo people, in the Sierra Nevada de Santa Marta, Colombia. The description of Wintukua politics allows for drawing some lessons of broader relevance. First, the Wintukua demonstrate that direct, deliberative democracy is practicable today. Second, we can gauge the importance of a common interest, which, in this case, is nurtured by shared cultural and religious practices. Finally, it appears that a strong focus on responsibilities, and not on rights, constitutes an important element to make direct, deliberative democracy among the Wintukua work.

Keywords: *Self-rule, deliberative democracy, First People, Colombia*

INTRODUCTION

The Wintukua is one of four indigenous groups living in the territory of the Sierra Nevada de Santa Marta, Colombia. The Sierra Nevada reaches a height of 5,775 meters above the sea and extends to the edge of the Caribbean. The Wintukua are about 50,000 people and tend to live in small settlements consisting of only a few households, on farms and 'fincas', that is: small, family farms. A minority lives in larger agglomerates – especially in *Nabusimake* the Wintukua capital and their holy city, which is about 2,000 meters above sea level in the heart of the Sierra. Along with the Wiwa, Kaggaba (Kogi) and Kankuamo peoples, the Wintukua live in an indigenous reserve, recognised by the Colombian state since 1980. The reservation is comprised of 661,527 hectares. Among these four groups, the Wintukua, known to the Non-Wintukua as the 'Arhuacos', are the largest and the best organised, giving them a leadership position among the four groups. In their own words, they are the 'older brothers'.

This essay is the result of empirical research with the Wintukuas, conducted between April and June of 2014, as well as consulting the existing literature.[1] I conducted open and semi-structured interviews with some Wintukua and Wiwa representatives and tribal members. My main interest was to learn more about Wintukua political organisation. Specifically, I sought to discover how collective decisions are made; how political rule is constituted; how political elites are selected and what role these political elites play in Wintukua political life.

I should explain that I am not trained as an ethnographer and that the ethnographic work informing this essay is scant at best. This is justifiable, in my mind, by the rather narrow research interest of this essay, which is restricted to unveiling the institutional dimensions of Wintukua political life. The methodology I chose reflects this interest, as well as my own academic training and experience as a political scientist interested in democratic institutions. This research is not based on extensive participant observation; instead, I sought answers to specific research questions in the most direct and efficient way possible, by asking Wintukua specialists and experts. I do not claim to be a specialist of the Wintukua people or of Colombian indigenous cultures – if such a specialisation exists (which I would find odd, as the most qualified specialists of Wintukua life are the same Wintukuas). Instead of presenting 'indigenous' or 'native' empirical material as a way to test, assess, or elaborate metropolitan theory, I instead seek to present Wintukua theory, Wintukua ontology, Wintukua epistemology and the Wintukua way of making sense of their world. To keep this exercise manageable, my focus is solely on political life, where politics, to me, is the exercise of collectively deciding how to live – and then institutionalising these decisions. However, as will become clear later on in the essay, the Wintukua way of conceptualising the political is not only different from Max Weber's, the structuralists, functionalists, and the Marxists; it is also different from my own.

While it certainly is important to understand different cultures in and on their own terms, I also want to argue that it is important to analyse different cultures and groups with the same analytical apparatus and from the same analytical angle as western, metropolitan cultures and groups have been analysed and to break the methodological division that so often divides studies of 'exotic' cultures from studies of 'modern' cultures. With this, I am engaged in a slightly different and probably more narrow enterprise than most subaltern scholars, such as Gayatri Spivak (1999), postcolonial feminists, such as Chandra Mohanty (1984), and de-colonial scholars, such as Walter Mignolo (2012, 2009, 2002). While these authors all rightfully warn against the application of western ontologies, epistemologies, explanatory models, and theoretical frameworks when attempting to analyse non-western cultures and their practices, in this essay, I consciously do just that: I want to demonstrate that even when applying western models, the Wintukua have something interesting to offer to all of us. In other words: the political contributions of the Wintukua to the world transcend their own culture and their emic values. Their political institutions, understood the same way as political institutions of complex western liberal democracies, are instructive, no matter what our cultural background.

I thus approach this field not as a cultural anthropologist and not as a post-colonial scholar, but as an American-trained political scientist and I argue that political scientists around the world can learn from Wintukua political institutions without having to first make themselves familiar with Wintukua culture. The insights we can gain from the Wintukua are thus no different, or less valuable, than those we can learn from ancient Athens, medieval city republics, Russian soviets, or American democracy.

While I take inspiration from all the authors mentioned above, I follow Sandra Harding, who has argued that 'we need realistic reassessments of both Western and non-Western knowledge systems' (Harding, 2008:6). For Harding, as for myself, this means that, 'if we are to take seriously the achievements of another culture, we have to talk about it in our terms, rather than theirs' (Harding, 2008:16).

My concerns are thus slightly different to those expressed by postcolonial scholars, most of whom seek to elevate the status of non-western thought and thus contribute to a 'provincialization of Europe' (Chakrabarty, 2007). I, instead, seek to demonstrate that no 'ethnic' lens is needed to recognise, and valorise the political institutions created, and maintained, by the Wintukua. In fact, I claim that mainstream political science falls prey to narrow eurocentrism if it only considers American and European political institutions. In other words: I want to argue that mainstream political science can no longer afford to ignore non-western democratic institutions and their potential answers to such universal questions as 'how to avoid elitism in political and economic life'.

With the essay, I thus want to contribute to a widening of the broadly accepted 'canon' of political institutions and hence thought, which to date only accepts western solutions to the problems of the world. In my mind, there is nothing 'special' about the proposals found in the work of Solon and Cleisthenes, as Cornelius Castoriadis (1991) and Slavoj Žižek (1998) want to make us believe – if 'special' refers to uniqueness. To me, the political reforms conducted by Solon, Cleisthenes, and Ephialtes are of interest the same way that other political institutions, proposed elsewhere and at other times with the same focus are interesting. They all help us address the apparently universal tendency towards elitism, that is, the ability of some individuals or groups to secure privilege for themselves.[2] In this, the solutions, and institutions devised by the Wintukua are as interesting, valuable, and deserving of our attention as those devised by the American Founding fathers.

The place where postcolonial critique and my own efforts converge most obviously is in the recognition that there are 'multiple modernities', (Chatterjee, 1998, 2001; Eisenstadt, 2000; Escobar, 2011). This view is that western, liberal democratic institutional solutions cannot claim to provide the only viable solutions to the universal problem of collective organisation and of how to broker power and control in fairness, freedom and equity. The Wintukua, to be sure, do not face the problem of having to decolonise their political, social, and economic lives. They have successfully done so over the past 500 years – by retreating deeper in and higher up the mountains and thus avoiding Colombian state power. In order to survive as a cultural entity, the Wintukua, similar to the other groups sharing the same reservation, have been engaged for centuries in what James Scott (2010) has termed 'agriculture of evasion'. In preserving their own ways, the Wintukua are practicing an alternative, non-metropolitan way to be modern, as none of their political institutions fall within the colonial framework of modern versus traditional, where 'traditional' in the colonial framework stands for 'primitive', 'backward', 'not-yet modern', and 'not-yet western'.

The Wintukua, to the contrary, have defined their own modernity – and it is a distinctively different modernity from the one sold wholesale by the likes of W.W. Rostow (1960), Samuel Huntington (1968), or Jeffrey Sachs (2006)

The political institutions created by the Wintukua and practiced by them today are also not a placeholder for any sort of larger tendency of Latin American Post-representational politics (Motta, 2014). They, in fact, share nothing with 'Latin' America – not even the same language. Wintukua political institutions are more akin to other native American and First People political institutions, to be found all over the Americas. With all of those, they share a concerted historical struggle for territory and autonomy (Dinerstein, 2014).

While I thus recognise the importance of 'border thinking' and 'double-translation' (Mignolo, 2002), the case at hand offers an opportunity to examine non-metropolitan political institutions without having to first rescue them from colonial misrepresentations and distortions – even if the Wintukua themselves face those and actively struggle against them. This approach has the advantage that one can escape the risk of constantly having to refer back to colonial power and thus, unwillingly, asserting its centrality (Esteva and Prakash, 1998).

POLITICAL INSTITUTIONS

Political institutions are central to all collective life. Human beings, because of their biological indeterminacy, have to invent, create and forge their collective lives into patterns and regularities in such a way as to allow for order and predictability. Only by creating institutions, that is, 'reciprocal typifications of habitualized actions', (Berger and Luckmann, 1966:72) are we able to free up enough mental capacities to respond creatively to a changing environment. Institutions, once created, give meaning to our social lives – and by doing so, they provide us with the means to order our own biographies and make sense of ourselves as parts of larger collectives. To a great extent, we are, as individuals, what we are as a group – and, conversely we are, as collectives, reflections of the institutions specific individuals have created to respond to, and address, specific problems (Berger and Luckmann, 1966).

Political institutions are a subset of social institutions as they were created to address a more narrow set of 'political problems', were politics, properly understood, is the ordering of collective life in terms of power and collective decision-making for the sake of justice, freedom, and equality (Castoriadis, 1990). Politics is all our business – even if some, western, institutional designers and their legitimations have wrestled politics away from 'the people' and made it the business of elites, supposedly 'representing' the people.

This essay is concerned with politics as defined here and political institutions in particular. I seek to demonstrate that Wintukua political institutions offer a particular solution to a universal problem. By examining Wintukua politics, I seek to recommend potentially promising political institutions that can be constructed elsewhere. Thus, while political problems are universal to the extent that all human collectives have to address problems of power, rule, justice, fairness, and equality, the solutions to these problems are manifold, giving room to the possibility of many modernities and much mutual learning. To think that western-type liberal democracy is the only possible answer to this universal problem is naïve, ignorant, euro-centric, and dangerous, as it leads to the formulation of western solutions for non-western problems. It is a colonial enterprise. Decolonisation instead points to the learning from, and with non-western institutions and by their assessment so that we can reach a global dialogue about which institutions serve whom the best, and under what conditions.

This is what I set out to do in this essay. I also hope to contribute to the effort by the Wintukua themselves who seek to gain recognition and respect from the Colombian government and the different national and international agencies potentially impacting their lives. As the Wintukua leader Mamo Kuncha Izquierdo explains: 'Knowledge is not owned by anyone in particular and as such should not be left in the care of an individual, much less for the sake of profit'. (Romero Infante and Barrios Guzmán, 2007: 57).

Guided by this principle, this essay argues that the way the Wintukua organise politically offers a viable alternative to the dominant ways of organising larger communities and societies, which post-war democratic theorists have typically argued are too complex to adopt participatory principles.

THE CRISIS OF COLLECTIVE POLITICAL AND ECONOMIC LIFE

On May 25, 2014, while conducting field research for this project, Colombia went to the voting booths to elect a new president. Of the 32,975,158 Colombians allowed to vote in the election, only 13,21,402 participated – some forty per cent of the electorate. The candidate with the most votes, Oscar Ivan Zuluaga, won 3.8 million votes – 29.3 per cent. The second most voted candidate, Juan Manuel Santos, received 3.3 million votes – 25.7 per cent of the total vote. Because of the lack of a majority, a second round of elections was held, leading Juan Manuel Santos to a second term. Juan Manual Santos rules over some forty-six million Colombians.

The Colombian electoral scenario is thus not very different from other countries calling themselves 'democracies'. Here as elsewhere, some sixty per cent of the population eligible to vote does not participate in the election of its executive and legislative leaders. Once elected, politicians of both the executive and the legislative body control the country for the time of their term, usually four years. They do this on behalf of the people, because, according to the parliamentary ideology, they represent them. This system, I seek to argue here, only works for those who wield power. In the parliamentary system, the 'people' do not practice democracy. They hand its exercise over to an elite who makes decisions on their behalf. All that is left for the people is to wait and hope that the decisions these elected rulers make are actually in their best interest. If not, all they can do is change them for other elites, four years later (Schumpeter, 1942).

In Colombia, the Gini coefficient for 2010 was 55.9, which placed the country at number ten of the most unequal countries in the world. Twenty per cent of the richest Colombians received 60.2 percent of the country's total income. On the other hand, the poorest twenty per cent received only three per cent of the country's income (World Bank, 2010). Wealth and asset holding is harder to assess, but must be thought of as even more skewed.

While Colombia is perhaps an extreme case in relation to many other countries, its disenchantment with politics, which finds expression in high electoral absenteeism and its high income concentration are global phenomena and characterise almost all formal 'democracies' of the world. Lessons learned from Colombia thus can be applied elsewhere (Castoriadis, 1998).

In most 'advanced' democracies today, the few practice democracy, claiming that they do so on behalf of the majority. The powerful few also concentrate economic power to the point that 'the rest' of us are left with precious little, precisely because the few take so much for themselves. This is so because under conditions of scarcity and limited resources characterising most markets, the gain of some is made possible by the loss of others. In competitive markets and under conditions of scarcity and limited resources, there is only one cake – and the rich eat it almost all by themselves. Under normal economic conditions, the more some gain, the more others will loose, where this tendency is path dependent, so that more gain in the past tends to lead to even more gain in the future. The rich not only get richer and the poor poorer; the rich can use their assets to protect and shield their riches and ensure bright futures to their offspring. They can also use their riches and apply them to politics, where they can shape the very institutions that allowed them to become rich in the first place. They can engage in 'opportunity hording' in the parlance of economists, while the poor can watch in awe the spectacle provided by powerful and rich political elites, supposedly done for the sake of the 'common good' (Hirsch, 1976; Frank, 2011). Most advanced democracies are thus neither advanced nor democratic – if democracy is taken by its original meaning: the rule of the people. Instead of equal opportunity, they offer a tiered economic system, where millionaires have long decoupled from 'the people' and compete among each other based on conspicuous consumption (Veblen, 1994), while middle and lower classes face ever increasing competition. What are the alternatives? We know that there are some – but Western epistemological hegemony does not allow us to see them (Sousa Santos, 2014).

As I want to show here, in a country like Colombia, the alternatives are practiced daily in the mountains, valleys, and deserts by communities who have managed to defend their autonomy so they can practice their own forms of political and economic organisation. Foremost, alternatives are practiced by natives, or Indians, who since 1991 have the right to political autonomy. The Wintukua are of particular interest because they have maintained many of their traditional political institutions and ways of organising, thus serving as a rich and informative single case study, offering valuable lessons on various aspects of community life.

INDIGENOUS PEOPLE IN COLOMBIA

The Colombian government recognises eighty-four indigenous or native groups, with a total population of 1,378,884 (DANE, 2012). Each group presents an interesting case of alternative ways to organise political, economic, social and cultural life, as all of them actively have been resisting colonial domination and sought to preserve political autonomy so they can practice their ancestral ways of organising political, social, economic, and cultural life. Indigenous people in Colombia have a long history of struggle and resistance. This began with the Spanish conquest and continues to the present. The Cacique Turmequé wrote a letter of protest to the King of Spain in 1584, which states:

> I can certify to Your Majesty that is true that there are no Indians more pursued, harassed, molested and poor, as the ones who have been put under your royal crown ... The wretched Indians do not know where to turn to seek redress of grievances because these are the facts. They can only cry to heaven and mourn their misfortune, because of the wrongs done to them, taking advantage of their wives and daughters, a particularly terrible cruelty done to those who are your people.
>
> (Sánchez Gutiérrez y Molina Echeverri, 2010: 392f, my translation)

Native Colombians thus can look back at an accumulated experience of struggle, which started in the sixteenth century and continues today. Their struggle is not only for physical survival, but for the cultural survival as a people. Thus, the focus of their struggle, since colonial times, has been for land, autonomy and the preservation of culture.

With the independence of Gran Colombia in 1819 the situation for the native peoples did not improve. Independence, however, resulted in an important declaration that is used to this day, called 'Order of the Liberator', by Simón Bolívar, who in 1820 ordered the return of Indian lands occupied by settlers:

Wishing to correct abuses introduced in Cundinamarca[3] on most of the
natural peoples against their liberties and considering that this part of
the population of the Republic deserves paternal care of the Government
for having been the most vexed, oppressed, and degraded during Spanish
despotism, with the presence of the provisions contained in canonic and civil
law, has thought proper to decree:
Essay 1. All of the lands that were previously held as reservations will be
returned to the natural people, no matter who the current holders.

(Sánchez Gutiérrez y Molina Echeverri, 2010:
ATTACHMENTS, my translation)

Despite many laws and regulations, the Spaniards and their descendants, now
Colombian citizens, flouted Bolivar's wishes and gradually invaded Indian reser-
vations, distributing their land among white and mestizo settlers. The Roman
Catholic Church played a central role in the submission and pacification of the
Indians, as they established missions in the reservations.

Under the law, Indians were treated as minors and were put under the tutelage
of missionaries who were responsible for them. This law also detailed 'how the
primitives (*salvajes*) should be governed and brought into civilized life' (Sánchez
Gutiérrez y Molina Echeverri, 2010:17, my translation). De jure and de facto, until
the new constitution of 1991, Colombian indigenous peoples were considered
minors, falling under the guidance of their governmental or ecclesiastical tutors
(Yrigoyen Fajardo, 2009). Laws such as law 89 of 1890 and Law 55 of 1905 aimed
at breaking up reservations and annihilate the Indians Cabildos, their governments,
forcing native people to assimilate and join the nation as individuals and opening
up their reservations to peasant settlement.

An important step in the history of indigenous resistance is linked to the name
Manuel Quintín Lame (1883-1967), 'who promoted a survey between 1914 and
1918 in the department of Cauca' (Sánchez Gutiérrez y Molina Echeverri, 2010:17,
my translation). Lame also formulated a programme that today serves as a reference,
the Lame Manifesto. It demands:

1.   The recovery of the reservations;
2.   The extension of the reservations;
3.   The strengthening the Cabildos;
4.   The non-payment of land property taxes (*terraje*);
5.   The dissemination of knowledge about indigenous laws and their fair
     application;

6.   The defense of indigenous history, language, and customs;
7.   The training of indigenous teachers.
(Sánchez Gutiérrez y Molina Echeverri, 2010:18, my translation)

Other highlights of indigenous struggles in Colombia are the formation of the CRIC – Regional Indigenous Council of Cauca – in 1971, and the formation of the National Indigenous Organisation, now called the National Authority for Indigenous Government of Colombia (ONIC), in 1982. While these organisations channelled indigenous struggle into coherent frameworks and allowed for the formulation of a broadly shared agenda, the Colombian state did not permit great advances.

With the constitution of 1991, finally, native Colombian peoples did, at least on paper, gain legal recognition and the right to political autonomy. The 1991 constitution demands the recognition and protection of ethnic and cultural diversity; recognition of the autonomy of indigenous groups and their own forms of government; affirmation of the inalienable character of indigenous territories and protection of the commons; protection of natural resources; and the creation of indigenous territorial entities within the territorial organisation of the nation.

WINTUKUA POLITICS

The 1991 Constitution of Colombia provides in its article 330 that 'indigenous territories shall be governed by councils formed and regulated according to the customs of their communities'. With this, the Colombian state recognises the customary laws of indigenous groups such as the Wintukua. In many cases, particularly among Andean native communities, this custom consists of the Cabildo, a municipal council organisation of Spanish origin. In Spain, and later in the Spanish Americas, settlers practiced Open Cabildos, a form of public assembly, which first appeared in Spain around the fifth to sixth centuries. Cabildos came to the Americas with the Spanish conquerors and settlers in the sixteenth century (Tapia, 1965; Bayle, 1952). This institution was subsequently lost in Spain and the American conqueror and settler communities – but it survived and gained new strength of expression among American indigenous societies and among Maroon city republics that also practiced different forms of direct democracy (Reiter, 2015). Thus, as white settlers moved from open councils to slavery and feudalism, Indians and runaway slaves integrated these participatory democratic institutions into their own governance institutions and by doing so ensured the survival of the Cabildo system. According to the Colombian Ministry of Interior,

> The Indigenous Council is a special public entity, whose members are members of the indigenous community, elected and recognised by it as a traditional socio-political organisation whose function is to legally represent the community, to exercise authority and perform the activities attributed to it by the laws, their customs and internal rules of each community. (my translation)

For Enrique Sánchez Gutiérrez and Hernán Molina Echeverri (2010):

> In the Andean region political authority rests in the Cabildos. Each reserve (or reservation) has its own council, and council members are elected periodically by members of the community. The role of the council is to organise the work, divide the available communal lands, settle internal disputes, and represent the reservation to the white authorities. The Cabildo was an institution imposed by the Spanish on the indigenous communities in the seventeenth and eighteenth centuries, but it was adapted to our interests and traditions. It has been one of the main instruments for the defense of indigenous communities and is key to the defense of reservation lands and the recovery of land stolen by landowners ... Experience has shown – both in northern Cauca and throughout the country – that the Cabildos are our best weapon to organise, to recover the land that we have been deprived of and to maintain and develop our community life. (Sánchez Gutiérrez and Molina Echeverri, 2010:215, my translation)

Parallel to the Cabildo structure, the Wintukuas have another internal structure, of sacred and wise people, who have great authority among the peoples of the Sierra: the *Mamos*. According to Romero Infante and Guzmán Barrios, the Wintukua 'administer themselves through a dual system between traditional authorities or Mamos and civil authorities or Cabildos, secretaries, commissioners, prosecutors and counselors. The Cabildos are elected by the Mamos in special councils and decisions are made in assembly considering the advice and words of the same Mamos' (Romero Infante and Guzmán Barrios, 2007:55, my translation).

This system of dual power was evident during my stay in Colombia. On May 17, 2014, the Wintukuas chose their new Cabildo governor, José María Arroyo. The process of choosing him followed the traditional model. First, the Mamos agreed on who should be the new governor. Seventy Wintukua Mamos, through numerous meetings and after several spiritual consultations, deliberated to the point where everyone agreed on the candidate. This process took several weeks. The selected candidate was then presented to the general assembly for discussion and approval. In the first phase, which in 2014 lasted for fifteen days, there was no vote but a deliberative process that extended to the point where all seventy Mamos agreed. Then there was a general assembly meeting, open to all community members. On this occasion, some 400 Wintukuas attending the general assembly decided whether to accept the candidate suggested by the Mamos. They also listened to the rendering of accounts given by the outgoing governor and to the proposals of the new governor to be.

To my question 'how many times does the general assembly meet?' the Wintukua representatives I interviewed explained, 'as often as necessary – whenever there is a decision to take or a project to approve'. They also explained that each investment and intervention project has to be approved by an internal deliberative process, followed by a process of discussion and approval at a general assembly. Margarita Villafaña, who is a Wintukua spokesperson, explains: 'We live apart, in families, but weekly, or monthly, depending on the need, we meet to make decisions. In these meetings in the villages, everyone has a voice, including women, youth and children. When we need to take major decisions that affect everyone, we hold a general assembly, with all the people (Interview in Santa Marta, June 1, 2014, my translation). The process, Moisés Villafaña, another Wintukua spokesperson, explains, has two stages: 'First, each village forms an assembly to discuss. Then, they communicate their decisions to the Wintukua authorities. After that, all the Mamos meet and finally the Mamos take their decision to the general assembly for discussion. That is when the final decision is made (Interview in Santa Marta, June 1, 2014, my translation).

The Wintukua political system is best characterised as deliberative and direct democratic, where legislative decisions are reached in public assembly. Assemblies, it is worth noting, are frequently held, whenever needed. Public assemblies are open to all, men, women, youth, and children and they are held at different levels: in villages or meeting places of the families residing in a region; between Mamos; and in general, mostly at the capital of Nabusimake, where all people attend.

My research also demonstrated that the citizenship of the peoples living in the Sierra de Santa Marta is active and full of responsibilities that extend beyond their own groups, because according to their worldview, they have a responsibility towards the world. Their culture thus contrasts sharply with the white and mestizo culture around them, because among those, citizenship is not built on the responsibilities, but based on rights. These rights come from the law and are not the result of a communal or social pacts or contracts.

THE MAMOS: POLITICAL LEADERS WITHOUT POLITICAL POWER ACCORDING TO MIGUEL ROCHA VIVAS (2010),

> The *mamus*, mamas or mamus, are priests, physicians, and community leaders who have different specialisations and ranks depending on their place of origin, community, descent, training, religious prestige, etc. In that sense, the mamos are the ultimate bearers of the original words, major words that after having been written down in Latin characters have come to be called myths, stories, songs, and what we call traditional literatures and wisdom, or *oralituras*, in reference to their origin and pre-eminently oral transmission.
>
> (Rocha Vivas, 2010: 503f, my translation)

Atí Saraí, a Wintukua woman, explains: 'A Mamo is already born Mamo. They come from Mamo families. Early on they are taught and their learning never ends. They must live a healthy lifestyle. They practice fasting. They have special regulations and food restrictions' (Interview in Santa Marta, May 17, 2014, my translation). The Mamos are the spiritual leaders of the Wintukua. They are their priests, guides and counsellors. They are leaders, but they are not representatives. They are counsellors, but they have no political power as even their input in the selection process of the Cabildo governor is merely advisory and the general assembly makes the final decision.

To become a Mamo, one has to be trained and prepared from youth. The future Mamos have to go through times of seclusion and meditation. They must follow stringent behavioural and dietary codes. They do not eat meat or salt. At the same time, the Mamos are the guardians of the sacred sites of the Sierra Nevada de Santa Marta. They are the interpreters and conduits for these sites, since it is through them and their interpretations that the community accesses these sites. Each Mamo is responsible for a different site. In a recorded meeting among different Wintukua, Wiwa and Kogi Mamos in 1980, held to resolve a dispute over sacred ground, we can read the following descriptions of the attending Mamos:

> Valencia Saravata, cacique Señor Don Arruenmaco, responsible for the custody of all the land of the father; Julian Inquimako, Don Señor of government, responsible for the custody of the internal and spiritual life, of nature and man; ... father Don Manuermo, charged with the custody and preservation of trees, rivers, animals and food; ... Prosecutor Pedro Inkimaco; ... signing are the Mamos Señor Don Dimarucua, chief secretary; Juan Jacinto Saravata, responsible for advising the Mamos among each other and to the community to

maintain harmony; ... Inkimaco Santiago, senior commissioner of Makotama; Pedro Avingue, commissioner of San Miguel; Benito Alimako, senior commissioner of San Francisco; Padilla Mamatakan, minor commissioner of San Francisco; José Sauna, commissioner of Moraka; Joaquin Alimako, commissioner of Pueblo Viejo; Ramon Gil Barros, Cabildo governor of the Kogi-Arsario; Manuel Alimako, commissioner of San Pedro; Adán Villafañe and Dionisio Villafañe, representatives of the Arhuaco Cabildo Governor.

(Sánchez Gutiérrez y Molina Echeverri, 2010: 88f, my translation)

This list sheds some light on the different responsibilities of each of the attending Mamos, Caciques, council commissioners, and governors. Similar to classical and medieval European republics, Wintukua citizenship is characterised primarily by duties and responsibilities. The more prestigious a Mamo, the greater his responsibilities.

In general, the responsibilities of the Wintukua reach far beyond their own community, because according to their beliefs, they are responsible for the world. In their view, the Sierra Nevada contains the whole world – it is the heart and navel of the world. In a complaint letter to the President of the Republic, dated July 7, 1968, the Mamo Vicencio Torres Marquez expressed a conviction that I heard a lot when talking to members of the four indigenous groups in the Sierra Nevada de Santa Marta: 'This place is the heart of all human beings who exist everywhere in the world' (Gutiérrez Sánchez and Molina Echeverri, 2010: 76, my translation). In the same letter, this important Mamo writes:

Of this consist our laws, religion and customs: those who belong to these tribes have to care for and assist all those mentioned sites and fulfil our duties in the work of our hidden and traditional science. That is our obligation. In this way, the highlands and mountains of the Sierra Nevada were made and from here the world spread to other places, before the daylight came. It was here that the mothers of the three kingdoms of nature resided, which are: the mineral kingdom, the plant kingdom and the animal kingdom.

(Sánchez Gutiérrez and Molina Echeverri, 2010:70, my translation)

The Mamos are, in the words of Moisés Villafaña, spiritual guides, counsellors, astrologers, and Wiseman. They do not give orders – they give advice. They also serve as judges for civil and criminal cases that do not involve non-Indians. For the Wintukua, bad behaviour, crime and other anti-social behaviours are the result of a spiritual problem of the person who caused it. It is part of the responsibility of a Mamo to identify the root of this problem and address it with the person. It is understood that the cause of a spiritual problem may be rooted in the past – including in the previous generations. If a problem occurs in this way, a Mamo guides the healing process, which, over time, also includes the party affected by any misbehaviour or crime. This usually consists of acts of restitution. Moisés Villafaña explains:

> For us, the conflict comes from a spiritual disease and you have to heal this disease. If not repaired, it will follow us. For us, unlike the Western system, the emphasis is not on punishment, but on restoring. It may also involve community work or work for the victim.
>
> (Interview in Santa Marta, June 1, 2014, my translation)

The Mamos thus are a different sort of leader. They lead by example and wield no political power. As leaders, they fall under strict behavioural codes and serve as living examples of conduct. The more prestige they carry, the more responsibilities they have. In other words: They could not be more different from the elected officials in 'modern' democracies. Among the Wintukua, all political power to make collective decisions rests with the different assemblies. Particularly the power to make rules and laws is shared among all members, even the young. In those assemblies, deliberation is practiced and collective decisions are reached through argument, persuasion, and listening to the opinions of others. Votes are taken only after much debate in case no agreement can be reached. To reach balance, equilibrium, and harmony are the explicit goals of Wintukua political life. To shed some light on the importance of balance in Wintukua life, a closer look at the institution of 'payments' is helpful.

THE PAYMENTS: RE-ESTABLISHING BALANCE AND HEALING THE WORLD

In the worldview of the Wintukua, harmony and balance play a central role. If the balance is broken, it needs to be restored. The Mamos know how to re-establish a lost balance. Margarita Villafaña explains:

> When someone commits an offense, we understand that this affects the whole environment; the victim and his family, but also the one who committed the crime and his family. If you do not treat it, it can affect the whole community and become a social problem. So what do we do? We start a process of healing that involves the victim's family and the family of the person who committed

the offense. We understand that this has its roots somewhere and a place where you can make a deposit and heal, so this does not happen again.

(Interview in Santa Marta, June 1, 2014, my translation).

Thus, the Mamos identify the problem, which is interpreted as a fracture of the balance, and they make recommendations in order to re-establish it. They also guide the process of re-balancing. In the Wintukua worldview, all imbalances have a local and territorial dimension and it is through these specific places that specific balances can be re-established. Once this work is done, other activities directly related to the individuals and groups involved with the loss of balance follow. The Mamos, now supported by the executive authorities of the Cabildo, also recommended compensatory actions for the victims of a violation.

Two common ways to break the balance are the abuse of power and the establishment of inequality. When asked, 'what do you do when one Wintukua wants to be richer and more powerful than the others', the two spokespeople explain: 'If this happens, we call an assembly'. In the traditional Indian practice and due to the fact that land titles given by the federal government to indigenous reservations are of collective nature, an individual person cannot own land. It may be that a family, out of habit, considers a land as belonging to this family, but in reality it is not theirs and can go back to the community at any time. At the same time, it is up to each family to take care of their ancestral land and each family has an ancestral land, containing a sacred site for just this family – a site that connects family members with their ancestors. They can never sell this land. They are only allowed to sell the surplus produced on this land – the fruit of their labour. At the same time, a family cannot have more land than needed and the community watches to achieve a balance between the families as a way to maintain equality among all. According to Margarita Villafaña, 'a few years ago the Wintukua began a process of land redistribution, because they realised that the lands of some families, because it was high up in the mountains, did not yield enough to feed their families' (Interview in Santa Marta, June 1, 2014, my translation).

Sacred sites play an important role in the process of re-establishing balance, as they are the doors to the spirit world and the healing process has to start on the spiritual level before it can be taken to the material level. In this process, the idea of distributive justice plays a central role: nothing is free. If we take something we need to put it back or replace it. Atí Saraí explains: 'If I say something, first I say: let me borrow it so I can talk. Therefore we say that everything in this life is borrowed and if someone wants it, she needs to pay for it' (Interview May 17, St. Martha, my translation). For the Wiwa, too, as Rocha Viva explains:

During payments or offering ceremonies and conciliations, the Mamos – the sages among the Wiwa – establish a quiet and focused dialogue with invisible beings in this and the other worlds. As money is used to pay bills, Mamos and sages use various materials to pay spiritually to the mysterious and countless parents of nature, which oraliteratura rather than religion – if they can be separated in this context – helps us visualise and sometimes understand. The Kogi Mamos tell us that they gave their writings to their 'little brothers'. Maria Sabina, a Mazatec sage, suggested that 'the book' can be viewed and read by those who have access to the deeper dimensions of spirit. In a joint statement, the Mamos said: [...] In Seynekun (are) the books shishi and pūnkūsa, which are books that contain the law, rules and functions of each of the species and ways to give back to the Fathers of each being, that is: the payments, the tributes.

(Fischer y Peuss, 1989: 92; Rocha Viva, 2010: 516f, my translation)

The principle of payments refers us to the sense of balance that must be maintained and, if disturbed, rebuilt. This balance is multifaceted, as it involves human beings, plants, rocks, lakes, rivers, animals and sacred sites. These are of central importance, because it is through the sacred sites that balance can be re-established, with payments. Thus, the relationship with the land and the sacred sites takes on a much more important connotation. They are the doors to other worlds.

WINTUKUA LAW

The Wintukua law is not a written law as Atí Saraí explains: 'The tree and the river are our law. The mountains and rivers are our code' (Interview in Santa Marta, May 17, 2014, my translation). According to the Kaggaba Mamo Arregocés Conchacala:

The words *site* or *sacred space*, are names we have given in Spanish to explain the extent of what they mean and represent. In our language (Kaggaba) these spaces are called *Jaba* and *Jate*, the parents of every one of the beings of nature and all that exists materially and spiritually. Sacred spaces give direction to planning and defining the categories of the system holistically. We do not plan in patches; our system is broader than the geographical borders of a valley.

(*Jaba and Jate*, 2012:5, my translation)

The magazine *Jaba y Jate* (2012), published by the Gonawindua Tayrona
Indigenous Organization (OGT) and coordinated by the Kaggaba Mamo
Arregocés Conchacala and the Kaggaba Cabildo Governor José de los Santos
Sauna, lists forty-nine *Jabas* and *Jates*, some of them containing other sites (such
as three sites at the mouth of the rivers in the Cienaga de Santa Marta and six sites
in Taganga), and four sacred sites currently outside of the reservation: Nakalindue,
Duanama, Jaba Segumain and Teguma – all in the region of the Sierra Nevada
Santa Marta. According to Arregocés Conchacala:

> The Sierra Nevada de Santa Marta is a sacred territory par excellence,
> composed by a large number of sacred sites. For the Kaggaba people, the Sierra
> is *Sé nenulang* – the physical and spiritual universe with all its components
> – and it contains the codes of the rest of the Earth. Africa, Europe, Asia, and
> Oceania are here and so are all oceans and all biodiversity, the stars, planets,
> galaxies in the universe represented in stones, tumas, hills and lakes. Protection
> and taking care of them also means protecting and taking care of everything
> that exists on the planet and in the universe.
>
> (*Jaba y Jate*, 2012:7, my translation)

It is worth noting: the world is represented in the stones, tumas, mountains, and
lakes. According to Mamo Conchacala:

> The Sierra Nevada de Santa Marta has its principles and fundamentals *Sé* or
> Law of Origin. This means that everything that exists has always existed mate-
> rially in spirit, to be the materialization of the world, everything has neat and
> clear functions. The order of the land and life forms are written in codes of
> nature: in lakes, stones, hills, in the birdsong and the sound of the breeze. Our
> Mamos know and spiritually handle these codes, which contain the alignments
> for education and proper training, for the organisation and maintenance of
> social welfare, for the balance of the environment, the protection of nature and
> all physical and spiritual existence.
>
> (*Jaba y Jate*, 2012:9, my translation)

Further:

> The Sierra Nevada de Santa Marta is the space designed from our origins as
> the Mother. It is the ancestral territory of the Kaggaba (Kogi), Arhuaco, Wiwa
> and Kankuamo peoples. It reflects the physical and spiritual universe, with all

its components and relationships, which together and in a well-articulated way, form a single living body demarcated by the so-called Black Line.

(Jaba y Jate, 2012:9, my translation)

The Sierra Nevada and the sacred sites she contains thus function as a whole and as a living organism. Nature is not, as in western thought, a mere substrate for life. For the Wintukua, Kaggaba, Wiwa, and Kankuamo, as for other natives of the Americas, nature *is* life. And it is a well-organised life, where every place has specific rules and functions. Each site contains a law. That *is* the law for the Wintukua, Kaggaba, Wiwa, and Kankuama. A law that is manifested in the territory. Reading, understanding, and interpreting this law is the central work of the Mamos and they are prepared for this task during their lifetime. According to Wiwa authorities:

The mother is also a transmitter of knowledge. From her comes the law of origin. The Mother transmitted her knowledge to her son Siokokui by 'a book', from which he learned and from which Wiwa life and thought developed; from which knowledge and the foresight where transmitted to communicate what can happen to any of us and to Nature [...] This knowledge includes the guidelines for the organisation of social and natural life, for the words and standards of behaviour and for the handling and timing of events of personal, family and community history; at the same time, these forms of communication were given to us so we can return them to the ancestors and to talk with them, to read and to hear their words [...] It is those same ancestors who make us remember. And they say: Wake up! Continue with your stories, your sages, your payments.

(Organisation Wiwa Yugumaiun Tairona Bunkuanarua, 2001: 120, 154, cited in Rocha Vivas, 2010: 508, my translation)

Thus, nature *is* the law. The problem is that many people are no longer able to read the book and understand nature and its laws. That is why we need the Mamos, because they have kept alive this capacity. The Colombian anthropologist Cristina Echavarría explains:

The Mamos are always saying that 'the birds do still as their mother told them, but we are already forgetting; we have to study the birds to remember and to do like them'(Echavarria, 1993: 221, my translation).

According to Wintukua thinking, which is very similar to the thinking of other groups living in the Sierra Nevada de Santa Marta, social and political life is not separate from the spiritual life and nature. If something happens in the life of an individual, it affects the community and it has spiritual and natural roots. For life to flow well, there must be balance between all these domains. Re-establishing a broken balance involves all levels affected by this imbalance. The healing process begins on the spiritual level, which, in turn, is anchored in nature, because nature *is* the spirit and it contains the broken law. In this view, there is no room for punishment and the focus is not on punishment, but on re-establishing a broken balance. To return to the law, sacred sites are key and the Mamos are the judges who preside over and guide this process.

CONCLUSION

Among the peoples of the Sierra Nevada de Santa Marta, the individual is closely connected to the community, or better: everything is connected. Sacred sites are interconnected – and if one is destroyed, the circle is broken and the system does not work anymore. The interconnection between the sacred sites is called the 'black line'. There can be no harmony or health if the black line is interrupted. No health or welfare in the Sierra or in the world. The welfare of the people is dependent on their environment – both personal and natural. A Wintukua explains:

> Public Health refers, in our worldview, to the work that the Mamos conduct [...] in order to maintain the balance of all beings who dwell on it based on the four elements fire, air, water and land ... In short, territoriality involves health, water, wind, and all the elements surrounding nature.
>
> (Romero Infante and Guzman Barrios, 2007:56, my translation)

The lives of the Wintukua and other peoples of the Sierra Nevada de Santa Marta is a life of severe political responsibilities. They feel responsible not just for the welfare of the Sierra – but the world. This sense of responsibility is reflected in their active and participatory citizenship. They gather in assemblies, choose representatives to communicate with the outside world, and follow the advice of their Mamos who are leaders, judges, counsellors, but *not* representatives. They bear an even heavier responsibility to the world because the re-establishment of broken balance is their responsibility.

The Wintukua choose executive leaders such as Sheriffs (*cabos*), commissioners, and governors – but they only do so to enter in dialogue with the outside world. Their internal political life is arranged by assemblies – both locally and at the level of the nation as a whole. In this, there are no representatives, as there is in the world of the whites and mestizos.

The life of these communities is a life of the word, of discourse, dialogue, and deliberation. Decisions affecting the community are taken together in deliberative processes that only end when consensus is reached – no matter how long it takes. At the same time, collective decisions are guided by the wise, who are not representatives, but leaders who give advice and provide living examples.

The political life of the natives of the Sierra Nevada de Santa Marta thus is an active political life, full of responsibilities, where the most prominent members carry more severe responsibilities. It is a life of deliberative and consensual politics, where every word is important. And it is a life where the political is connected to the religious and the cultural, as it is from the cultural and religious life that the rules and norms of individual and collective behaviour come from.

Hence, Wintukua politics could not be more different from the political life of the white world. Instead of voting, Wintukua have deliberation and consensus. Instead of rights, they have responsibilities. Instead of capitalism and profit, they have community and collective ownership of land. Instead of the analytical and ontological separation of the world into sacred and profane worlds they have one world where the sacred influences the profane, where the spiritual world is connected to the material world and where everyone is anchored in the natural world.

If we believe such authors as Bernard Manin (1987), who argues that the legitimacy of democracy is not in the ballot, but in deliberation – then we can see that the Wintukua have a much more advanced democracy than the white and mestizo people around them. That should also be the conclusion when we consider the argument of Jane Mansbridge (1980), who explains that modern democracy is an adverse, cynical democracy that replaced the common interest by selfish interest. Other authors who criticise modern democracy in this way include Jean Jacques Rousseau (2003), Hanna Pitkin (2004), Hannah Arendt (1965, 1973) and Cornelios Castoriadis (1990, 1998, 2001).

Instead of a minimalist and elitist democracy, which is the democracy of 'civilized' Colombia – the Wintukua practice deep democracy, which includes everyone and is based on a strong and active citizenship – similar to the citizenship of ancient Athens, the free city republics of medieval Europe and the Maroon republics founded on Colombian territory around the year 1600 (Arrázola, 1970). The Wintukuas, like the Maroons, have given continuity to the Spanish tradition of the Cabildo, an open and democratic form of self-government, while the Spaniards and their descendants have fallen into feudalism, elitism, and cynicism. They demonstrate, in practice, that deliberative democracy is possible and viable in a rural, widely dispersed community of some 50,000. They also demonstrate that democracy can be based on consensus and mutual interest, along the lines Jane Mansbridge (1980) argues – and does not have to be adverse. Democracy, it appears, requires community and community must be based, in part, on mutual interest. Among the Wintukua, it seems that their cultural and religious practices provide the glue that hold their community together, or, put stronger: it is their cultural and religious practices that makes them Wintukua and they are only able to live together and organise their political life as long as they all share a Wintukua identity.

Another important lesson we can learn from Wintukua political life concerns their strong emphasis on responsibilities over rights. Not once did any of the Wintukua, Wiwa, Kogi, or Kaggaba I spoke to mention anything about their 'rights'. Their focus was firmly on responsibilities; responsibilities toward the collective, toward nature – even toward human kind. Rights, if at all present, are collectively constructed and upheld – not codified and legally enforced among tribal members, but here, as elsewhere, the principle of harmony and equilibrium seem the guiding principles, overseen by their Mamos.

From the Mamos we can learn how political leaders can look like; how responsible they can live and act; and how they can serve as examples and inspirations, without actually wielding effective power. The power to make binding collective decisions, it is worth highlighting again, rests with the assemblies and with this, Wintukua self-rule is guaranteed. Administrative functions are given to elected officials – but they have no legislative power, thus following the important separation of political from administrative power highlighted by some anarchist scholars (Bookchin, 2015). The most important lesson we can all learn from the Wintukua, it seems to me, is that self-rule and direct democracy are possible today – even if some elements of the way how the Wintukua practice their self rule are determined by their own history and culture, thus giving it a specific, Wintukua, dimension. This is, after all, how we expect self-rule to emerge and develop: out of local traditions and embedded in a specific local culture and responding to specific challenges posed by concrete, historical as well as spatial constellations.

Bernd Reiter is a professor of comparative politics at the University of South Florida. His work focuses on citizenship and democracy. His publications include *The Crises of Liberal Democracy and the Path Ahead* (forthcoming with Rowman and Littlefield), *Bridging Scholarship and Activism* (2015), *The Dialectics of Citizenship* (2013), among others.

NOTES

1. For example, Arango y Sánchez, 1998; Barragán y Marino, 2005; Mejía Gutiérrez, 1973; Sánchez Gutiérrez y Molina Echeverri, 2010.
2. Robert Michels (1966) [1911] found that elitism and oligarchy were the inevitable outcomes of formal organizational structures, as, inevitably, one group will take leadership positions within any organisation and thus wield more power than the common members. The only ways out of this dilemma, it seems to me, are to either not allow formal organizational structures to consolidate; to constantly devise new structures that work against a consolidation of power in a few hands; or to devise institutional barriers that smartly block the formation of elites. It is this third strategy that seems most promising and worth examining here.
3. The province of Cundinamarca initially resisted the independence forces. Simón Bolivar let the military expedition to punish Cundinamarca and force them to join the cause.

REFERENCES

Arango, Raúl y Enrique Sánchez 1998. *Los Pueblos Indígenas de Colombia*, Bogotá: Tercer Mundo Editores.

Arendt, Hannah 1973. *The Origins of Totalitarianism*, New York: Harcourt, Brace, Jovanovich.

_____ 1965. *On Revolution*, New York: Penguin.

Arrázola, Roberto 1970. *Palenque, primer pueblo libre de América. Historia de las sublevaciones de los esclavos de Cartagena*, Cartagena: Ediciones Hernández.

Barragán Pardo, Julio Marino (ed.) 2005. *Mamalwa: Modelo Ancestral de Ordenamiento Territorial Indígena, Cuenca del Rio Santa Clara, Sierra Nevada de Santa Marta*, Santa Marta: Dibulla.

Bayle, Constantino 1952. *Los Cabildos Seculares en la América Española*, Madrid: Sapientia, S.A. de Ediciones.

Berger, Peter and Thomas Luckmann 1966. *The Social Construction of Reality*, New York: Penguin Books.

Bookchin, Murray 2015. *The Next Revolution*, New York: Verso

Castoriadis, Cornelius 2001. 'The Retreat from Autonomy: Post-modernism as Generalised Conformism', *Democracy & Nature*, Vol. 7, No. 1, (2001): 17-26.

_____ 1990. 'What Democracy?' in *Figures of the Unthinkable*, Open Manuscript.

_____ 1991. 'Aeschylean Anthropogony and Sophoclean Self-Creation of Man', in *Figures of the Unthinkable*, http://www.notbored.org/FTPK.pdf.

_____ 1998. *The Imaginary Constitution of Society*, Cambridge: MIT Press.

Chakrabarty, Dipesh 2007. *Provincializing Europe*, Princeton: Princeton University Press.

Chatterjee, Partha 2001. 'On civil and political society in post-colonial democracies', in Kaviraj, Sudipta and Sunil Khilnani (eds) 1998. *Civil Society*, Cambridge: Cambridge University Press, pp165-178.

_____ 1998. *A Possible India*, Oxford: Oxford University Press.

Dinerstein, Ana C. 2014. *The Politics of Autonomy in Latin America The Art of Organizing Hope*, Jude Howell (ed.), Hampshire: Palgrave MacMillan

Dussel, Enrique 2012. 'Philosophy of Liberation, the Postmodern Debate, and Latin American Studies', in Morana, Mabel, Enrique Dussel, and Carlos Jaurequi (eds) 2008. *Coloniality at Large*, Durham: Duke University Press, pp335-249.

Echavarría Usher, Cristina 1993. *Cuentos y cantos de las aves tairona, mitología ornitológica wiwa*, Medellín: Corporación Murundúa y Colciencias.

Eisenstadt, S.N. 2000. 'Multiple Modernities', *Daedalus*, 129.1 (Winter 2000): 1-29.

Escobar, Arturo 2011. *Encountering Development*, Princeton: Princeton University Press.

Esteva, Gustavo and M.S. Prakash 1998. *Grassroots Post-Modernism*, London: Zed Books.

Frank, Robert 2011. *The Darwin Economy*, Princeton: Princeton University Press.

Friede. Juan 1963. *Problemas Sociales de los Arhuacos*, Monografía, Facultad de Sociología. Bogotá: Universidad Nacional de Colombia.

Harding, Sandra 2008. *Sciences from Below*, Durham: Duke University Press.

Hirsch, Fred 1976. *The Social Limits to Growth*, Cambridge: Harvard University Press.

Huntington, Samuel 1968. *Political Order in Changing Societies*, New Haven: Yale University Press.

Manin, Bernard 1987. 'On Legitimacy and Political Deliberation', *Political Theory*. 15(3): 338-368.

Mansbridge, Jane 1980. *Beyond Adversary Democracy*, Chicago: Chicago University Press.

Mejía Gutiérrez, Jaime 1973. *Los Arhuacos*, Manizales: Universidad Nacional.

Michels, Robert 1966 [1911]. *Political Parties*, New York: Free Press.

Mignolo, Walter 2012. 'The Geopolitics of Knowledge and the Colonial Difference', in Morana, Mabel, Henrique Dussel, and Carlos Jaurequi (eds) 2008, *Coloniality at Large*, Durham: Duke University Press, pp225-258.

_____ 2009. 'Epistemic Disobedience, Independent Thought and De-Colonial Freedom', *Theory, Culture & Society*, 26 (7-8):1-23.

_____ 2002. 'The Zapatistas's Theoretical Revolution', *Review (Fernand Braudel Center)*, Vol. 25, No. 3 Utopian Thinking (2002):245-275.

Mohanty, Chandra Talpade (1984). 'Under Western Eyes: Feminist Scholarship and Colonial Discourses', *Boundary 2* (12:3-13:1): 333-358.

Morana, Mabel, Enrique Dussel, and Carlos Jaurequi (eds) 2008. *Coloniality at Large*, Durham: Duke University Press.

Sara C. 2012. 'Leyendo el anarchismo a traves de ojos latinoamericanos: Reading

Anarchism through Latin American Eyes', in Kinna, Ruth (ed.) 2014, *The Bloomsbury Companion to Anarchism*, London: Bloomsbury, pp252-277.

Odorozco, Jose Antonio 1990. *Nabusimake: Tierra de Arhuacos*, Bogotá: ESAP.

Organización Indígena Gonawindua Tayrona 2010. *Jaba y Jate: Espacios Sagrados del Territorio Ancestral de Santa Marta*, Santa Marta: Duvan Silvera.

Pitkin, Hanna Fenichel 2004. 'Representation and Democracy: Uneasy Alliance', *Scandinavian Political Studies*, Vol. 27. No. 3 (2004): 335-342.

Plato 2002. *The Republic*, Available online at: http://www.idph.net.

Popper, Karl 1971 [1945]. *The Open Society and Its Enemies*, Princeton: Princeton University Press.

Reiter, Bernd 2015. 'Palenque de San Basílio: Citizenship and Republican Traditions of a Maroon Village in Colombia', *Journal of Civil Society*, Vol. 11, Issue 4 (2015): 333-347.

Rocha Vivas, Miguel (ors) 2010. *Antes el Amanecer: Antología de las Literaturas Indígenas de los Andes y la Sierra Nevada de Santa Marta*, Bogotá: Ministerio de Cultura.

Romero Infante, Jaime Alberto y Joaquin Alberto Guzman Barrios 2007. 'Administración ambiental del pueblo Wintukua, un ejemplo de colaboración Universidad El Bosque – Resguardo Indígena', *Cuadernos Latinoamericanos de Administración*, Vol. II No. 4 (Enero-Junio de 2007): 50-64.

Rostow. W.W. 1960. *The Stages of Economic Growth: A Non-Communist Manifesto*, Cambridge: Cambridge University Press.

Rousseau, Jean Jacques 2003 [1762]. *The Social Contract*, Judith Masters and Roger Masters (trans.), New York: St Martins Press.

Sachs, Jeffrey 2006. *The End of Poverty*, New York: Penguin Books.

Sánchez Gutiérrez, Enrique y Hernán Molina Echeverri (org) 2010. *Documentos para la historia del movimiento indígena colombiano contemporáneo*, Bogotá: Ministerio de Cultura.

Schumpeter, Joseph 2008 [1942]. *Capitalism, Socialism, and Democracy*, New York: Harper.

Scott, James 2010. *The Art of Not Being Governed*, New Haven: Yale University Press.

Sousa Santos, Boaventura 2014. *Epistemologies of the South: Justice against Epistemicide*, New York: Paradigm Publishers.

Spivak, Gayatri 1999. *A Critique of Postcolonial Reason*, Cambridge: Harvard University Press.

Tapia, Francisco Javier 1965. *Cabildo Abierto Colonial*, Madrid: Ediciones Cultura Hispánica; Torres Arroyo, Alberto. Sin fecha. *Yukweyna*, Santa Marta: Resguardo Arhuaco de la Sierra.

Veblen, Thorstein 1994. *The Theory of the Leisure Class*, London: Dover.

Yrigoyen Fajardo, Raquel 2009. 'De la tutela indígena a la libre determinación del desarrollo, la participación, la consulta y el consentimiento', *El Otro Derecho* No. 40 (jun, 2009): 11-48.
Žižek, Slavoj 1998. 'A Leftist Plea for "Eurocentrism"', *Critical Inquiry*, Vol. 24, No. 4 (Summer, 1998): 988-1009.

Anarchist Studies 25.1 © 2017 ISSN 0967 3393

www.lwbooks.co.uk/journals/anarchiststudies/

REVIEWS

Chris Ealham, *Living Anarchism: José Peirats and the Spanish Anarcho-Syndicalist Movement*

Oakland and Edinburgh: AK Press, 2015; 336pp; ISBN 9871849352383

With his biography of José Peirats Valls, the Herodotus of the Spanish anarchist movement, Chris Ealham has cemented his reputation as a leading authority in the field. His previous publications were significant contributions to the English language study of the topic. With this latest work, a superb biography of Peirats, he continues to add to our understanding. In just over 200 thoroughly documented pages (with over 1300 endnotes) Ealham has restored a man to his historical significance in the context of a full life spent in exceptional circumstances.

Peirats was born in a small Valencian village in 1908 and moved to Barcelona before he was four years old. From the age of six he suffered from Perthes Disease, a painful condition in his left femur. Peirats left formal schooling at age nine to become a brick maker, the occupation that Peirats proudly claimed until his death. Upon finishing his training, he formally became a member of the *Confederación Nacional del Trabajo* (CNT) at age twenty-two. His involvement with groups of neighbourhood youths evolved into an anarcho-syndicalist militancy and lifelong commitment to the CNT. Peirats became a prominent journalist and editor in the confederal press during the Second Republic and the Civil War. In 1937, he resigned from his editorial responsibilities and joined the Republican Army's 26th Division and on 10 February 1939, along with the rest of the Division, he went into exile in France. A brief period in a French concentration camp was followed by exile in the Dominican Republic, then Ecuador, Panama, and finally Venezuela. He returned to France in March 1947 where he lived and wrote *La CNT en la revolución española*, his magnum opus. He remained in France until he was able to return to his natal village in the 1980s. Diving into the Mediterranean, Peirats died in August 1989.

In a successful fusion of social history with biography, Ealham uses Peirats' personal experiences to examine the harsh reality for the Barcelona working class.

Throughout, Ealham's portrayal is sympathetic yet has a keen appreciation of the changes in the world that Peirats did not absorb. Ealham deftly places the Peirats family's precarious existence in the context of Barcelona before the Civil War and José Peirats' experience of conflicts within the CNT and FAI (*Federación Anarquista Ibérica*) through the war and into exile. Peirats wrote a great deal, but the richness of his ideas and opinions is contained in his correspondence and unpublished memoirs. Ealham has ably mined his massive archive (nearly two yards, principally of correspondence) and it enables him to provide Peirats' opinions, thoughts, and regrets throughout the biography.

Ealham has broken new ground in English language scholarship in his sobering and sad yet thorough account of the tribulations of both Peirats and the exiled Spanish anarchists. It is a sordid tale of expulsions, charges and counter-charges, and persecution of a number of sincere militants who disagreed with the organisation's direction under Federica Montseny and Germinal Esgleas. Ealham is harsher about pre-exile Montseny than I suspect Peirats was himself at that specific period of his life, though Ealham's view is one that is well-founded and expressed by many at the time. I am just not sure it was the view of Peirats in the early 1930s, though undoubtedly it was his view later in his life – and for excellent and well-founded reasons.

Please support anarchist publishing of such high quality and purchase this book – at about one pence per footnote, it is a steal.

Andrew H. Lee, Associate Curator, New York University

Davide Turcato (ed.), *The Method of Freedom: An Errico Malatesta Reader*
Edinburgh: AK Press, 2014; 530pp; ISBN 9781849351447

Malatesta is one of the best-known activists and writers in the 'canon' of anarchism. Several pamphlets and collections of his material have been published in English over the last several decades, especially by Vernon Richards and Freedom Press, but Turcato's edited volume offers a wider range of Malatesta's writings, improves upon earlier translations (aided by Paul Sharkey), and really gets across a sense of the evolution of Malatesta's ideas. The key aspects of this trajectory are condensed into *The Method of Freedom*, which precedes the eventual publication of a ten volume *Complete Works of Malatesta*, also on AK Press (volume three, the first to be published, was released in January 2017).

The newspaper articles and correspondences selected here present Malatesta in the shifting contexts of revolutionary agitation, from the First International, through several periods of exile in Argentina and London, to the Red Weeks, and eventually the rise of fascism in Italy. The selections also portray Malatesta's ideas as developing in antagonistic exchange with other writers of the time, and as reacting to developments in anarchist thought and praxis. The first of these developmental tensions was within the International Working Men's Association (IWMA) between Bakuninist collectivism and the emergent dominance of anarcho-communist ideas. Malatesta was certainly of the communist persuasion, arguing that 'collectivism is flawed in its moral foundation' and 'is incompatible with *anarchy*' (p47), but typifying his characteristic pragmatism, Malatesta argued early on that collectivism might be implemented in some areas on a 'transitional basis' (p47), to allow time for the collectivists to see the benefits of communist organisation of production. But as the dispute between collectivists and communists became drawn out, Malatesta took what Turcato describes as a 'pluralist stance' (p67) and argued for 'union between communists and collectivists' (p95) – such ideological bickering was senseless, because in his view (and providing the title for the book) 'Anarchy [is], above all, a method' (p141).

Malatesta also reacted to the emergence of anarcho-syndicalism, and though he was initially wary of trade unions and regarded 'an authentic general strike as unachievable' (p107), he was tentatively supportive, recognising that '[w]hatever may be the practical results of [economic] struggle ... [t]he revolutionary cause ... must benefit by the fact that workers unite and struggle for their interests' (p287). But he maintained a warning that syndicalism risked becoming 'an end in itself' and that it 'contains in itself, by the very nature of its function, all the elements of degeneration which corrupted Labour movements' (p339).

Turcato identifies 'an original gradualist view' (p267) emerging in Malatesta's thought during his exile in the United States after the 1898 bread riots in Milan. The theme of gradualism recurs throughout the selected writings from then onwards, but is explicated more and more clearly towards the end of Malatesta's life. As he put it: 'I believe that one must take all that can be taken, whether much or little: do whatever is possible today, while always fighting to make possible what today seems impossible' (p509). Turcato rephrases this nicely on the book's cover: 'our ends should not be disconnected from our action; our ideals should not be so lofty as to make no difference to what we do here and now' (back cover).

Malatesta was assuredly atheist and anti-clerical, but it is striking that his language often borrows from religious terminology, phrases such as 'holy', 'salvation' and 'sacred' crop up often, and indeed, he presented his anarchist philosophy as one rooted in love (p518). He was also unfailingly modest, and, as he became an elder grandee of the anarchist movement, rebuked those who 'inflicted' deference upon him, preferring to remain 'a comrade among comrades' (p395). The views of the older Malatesta are among the most interesting here, including recollections of Kropotkin after his death (p520) and critical reflections on the First International, sixty years on (p527).

There is a firm commitment to historical 'documentary accuracy' (p4) in this collection, with all writings being presented in their entirety, and translations corrected for fidelity to the original versions. This inevitably leads to some repetition of ideas across the selections, but the light-touch approach to the editing and framing of Malatesta's writings is surely an advantage. (For a more analytical approach to Malatesta, see David Turcato's *Making Sense of Anarchism* (AK Press, 2015)). This is a beautifully produced tome which makes an important contribution to our understanding of a seminal figure in the history of anarchism.

Jim Donaghey, Queen's University Belfast

Jesse Cohn, *Underground Passages: Anarchist Resistance Culture 1848-2011*

Edinburgh, Oakland, Baltimore: AK Press, 2014; 421pp; ISBN 9781849352017

With this wide-ranging and highly informative book, Jesse Cohn gives the reader an understanding of what culture has meant for anarchists in many of the numerous locales in which anarchist ideals have put down roots. The analysis extends from the time of Proudhon to the present, and from Europe and Russia to both American continents, with various references to the Far East. The book's deceptively simple primary questions are: 'How has anarchist resistance, global both in its aspirations and in its movements, been *translated* into the local vernacular of particular cultures and historical situations, *adapted* to the constraints of the genres and media available? Is there anything uniquely or consistently *anarchist* about the variety of cultural forms that some seven generations of anarchist men and women have happened to create?' (p22). This is explored in three sections, dealing with voice, the word, and the image – poetry and music; literature; illustration, graphic narrative and cinema.

Cohn switches constantly between different times and places, always focusing on what is specifically anarchist in cultural manifestations in contexts so distant from each other as to seem almost entirely unrelated. A number of constants emerge. Art for art's sake is out of the equation – the role of anarchist culture is to '*prefigure* a world of freedom and equality' (pp16-17). But art's propaganda value does not imply the production of unoriginal, strictly pedagogic works. Quite the contrary, as Cohn's fast-paced analysis of Brazilian poets, early Chinese science fiction writers, French popular storytellers, Catalan dramatists, Swiss illustrators, Spanish movie-makers, American comic artists, and (much) more, shows that the forms taken by the anarchist worldview can be both varied and surprising. Within this vast, painstakingly researched work, each reader will discover authors of whose existence s/he was never aware.

Cohn excels at using diverse theoretical approaches, without ever letting theory take centre stage, and the greatest value of this book is probably its comparative aspect. One conclusion in particular deserves highlighting: the supposedly 'banal' nature of anarchist literary creation, resistant to the lure of avant-garde 'originality', actually hides an unconventional use of conventions that comes across as a crucial element of unity. Tropes are hijacked, symbols are appropriated and traditions are both used and diverted. Defamiliarisation reigns. Caricature is omnipresent. Standard plots are used and abused freely, melodrama first of all. Generic plasticity is put to good use by writers who just don't know enough to know that, according to literary theory, they should not be able to find spaces of freedom within set narrative frameworks. Also constant is the tendency to reduce abstractions (class, the institutions, power) to characters; to embody them, providing an immediate representation of their function and reducing their appeal, demystifying them through representation in (often ridiculous, pitiful) flesh and bone. In opposition to this individualisation of the enemy, anarchist culture often 'enacts a we', stimulates the creation of a 'collective identity' (p146), and values like 'intimacy, contact, empathy' (p256) are underscored.

This is a book that should be essential reading for anyone interested in the relationship between anarchism and culture. Cohn proves the importance of the reflection on culture and its uses within the anarchist movement from its very beginning, showing the hollowness of the accusations of anti-intellectualism that have often been brought against it. And he also shows that anarchist culture is not a thing of the past, but an attitude and an approach that is still producing works that are worthy of critical attention in many genres and modes.

Vittorio Frigerio, Dalhousie University

The Invisible Committee, *To Our Friends*

Cambridge, MA: MIT Press, 2015; 240pp; ISBN 9781584351672

The Invisible Committee have returned! There is plenty to be sceptical about in *To Our Friends'* 239 pages, and in turn its authors waste no time in casting variously the left, radicals, Marxists, anarchists, hackers and pacifists alike as neither effective nor revolutionary. However, perhaps the best way to read this book, and indeed the way it is intended to be read, is as a set of challenges, concepts and confrontations demanding a response. Many of the revelations, analyses and statements contained within will resonate and it is easy to feel energised by the call to join the project of radical political and self-analysis they have begun here.

The book proceeds from the premise that what is first required today is a fresh diagnosis of our 'situation', one which would enable us to understand the collapse of the insurrections presaged in *The Coming Insurrection* and begin to resist more effectively. Revolution is the ultimate objective here, and anyone sharing this might consider themselves among the eponymous 'friends'. The influence of the French poststructuralists is heavily present and in many ways the book appears as an update or practical application of Foucault's work on biopower and governmentality, or Deleuze's societies of control and the model of the nomadic war machine, to name two obvious influences (though terminology is thankfully kept accessible). The world has changed, they tell us, and we have not yet managed to adapt.

The first argument in the book, that power no longer resides in institutions but in infrastructures, certainly seems compelling given recent struggles such as the TAV, Dakota Access Pipeline, Le ZAD, and Gezi Park. Governance, they claim, is in organisation. The cybernetic 'subject' emerges here, traceable across sensitive points where it connects with the machinery of flows – when we share our location with Google, when we enter our pin number, or when our number plate is noted on a 'smart' motorway. For this form of governmentality, surveillance no longer serves the purpose of monitoring individuals ('statistical entities don't take offence') and herein, we are told, lies the fallacy which has belied the revolutionary potential of every Western movement from Occupy to Anonymous: the freedom of the individual is no longer a viable battleground.

Concomitant to this, state politics has largely been replaced by crisis management techniques. Rather than marking the coming ultimate crisis of capital, this development has allowed capitalism to increase its evolutionary power. What is required for resistance, therefore, is a turn away from ideological inflexibility and an attention to place and community. The reason, they claim, that so many anarchists were left behind in the unfolding Greek riots is that the situation must create its people, not the other way around. Beyond the impotence of the general assembly, something more fundamental is occurring – the inhabitation of space. Thus, the blockade not the strike is the most effective corollary to insurrectionary action. Block the flows, disrupt the chains of social production. The book proceeds to lay a critique at the feet of radicals and pacifists, twin weaknesses – both aspire to purity – and numerous examples are given of how war/peace and radicality as standards have caused real practical problems for movements. This highlights a strength of the work: its willingness to give practical answers to the questions it poses.

After the impact of *The Coming Insurrection* there can be no doubt that the authorities will be reading this one – the book is an explicitly public project, translated into many languages and printed en masse. As propaganda, then, the choice of what to include and the form of the language is done with an awareness that this too is a text that will be monitored and adapted to.

Elizabet Vasileva, Loughborough University

Michael Knapp, Anja Flach and Ercan Ayboga, *Revolution in Rojava: Democratic Autonomy and Women's Liberation in Syrian Kurdistan,* translated by Janet Biehl

Chicago: University of Chicago Press, 2016; 272pp; ISBN 9780745336596 (paperback), 9780745336640 (hardback)

Since 2012, a self-professedly anti-state, anti-capitalist, democratic and feminist revolution has been under way in Rojava, northern Syria. It has received significant attention from anarchists, with some supporting it, others critiquing it, and a few travelling to Syria to join it. Unfortunately, English speakers interested in the revolution have largely had to rely on the internet as a source of information and so have been limited in what they can learn. *Revolution in Rojava: Democratic Autonomy and Women's Liberation in Syrian Kurdistan* helps to change this situation by providing a highly detailed and accessible introduction to the topic.

The authors draw primarily upon their own experiences of the region, interviews and discussions they have conducted with participants, and texts produced by the movement itself to present an overview of everyday life in Rojava and the history of the revolution. The result is that the authors manage to successfully combine an overarching sense of what is happening with how different individuals have personally experienced these events on the ground.

The book is arranged into fifteen chapters. It begins with two chapters on important context for the revolution, such as the history of Syria and the many different ethnic and religious groups in Rojava. This is especially useful for outsiders not familiar with the history of the region. From there the book goes on to describe different aspects of the revolution and the new society being built in Rojava. Topics include democratic structures, women's liberation, the economy, armed self-defence, ecological problems, and the education, healthcare and justice systems.

Of particular interest is the chapter on 'democratic autonomy' which details Rojava's practice of having bottom-up, directly democratic councils existing along-side top-down administrations run by elected representatives. Most surprising from an anarchist point of view is that the councils existed first and then voted to create new kinds of top-down structures known as Democratic-Autonomous Administrations. We are told that, so far, the bottom-up and top-down structures are managing to co-operate with one another, despite there not being a formal framework for how these relations should occur. Whether or not this co-operative relationship continues or fractures will have interesting implications for anarchist theory on prefiguration.

Also noteworthy is the chapter on the economy, which is one of the few detailed overviews of the topic available in English. It describes the revolutionaries' aim of a 'social economy' based on democratic self-management, and the concrete steps they are taking to achieve this goal, such as the creation of networks of co-ops and the redistribution of formerly state-owned land.

While the authors are active supporters of the revolution, they do not focus only on its successes. They frequently draw the readers' attention to challenges facing the revolution, problems which have not been overcome, and questions which are yet to be adequately answered. For example, due to the war and an embargo on Rojava there are great difficulties in creating sufficient healthcare and waste disposal systems.

Overall, I found *Revolution in Rojava* to be a useful source of information on the topic and an inspirational demonstration of what revolutionary forces can achieve in the twenty-first century. It is for both these reasons that I recommend it.

Oscar Addis, Loughborough University

Osvaldo Bayer, *The Anarchist Expropriators. Buenaventura Durruti and Argentina's Working-Class Robin Hoods,* translated by Paul Sharkey

Oakland and Edinburgh: AK Press, 2015; 160pp; ISBN 9781849352239

This newly-translated edition of Bayer's *The Anarchist Expropriators* is published by AK Press in collaboration with the Kate Sharpley Library and includes an introduction and timeline of events provided by the Kate Sharpley Library. This short book presents a series of vignettes focussing on events or characters in Argentina's history of anarchist bank-robbers between the end of the nineteenth century and the mid-1930s. As the introduction notes, 'Bayer's work belongs to the first wave of modern anarchist historiography that was, and still is, concerned with excavating anarchism's stories' (p1).

This approach lends the book a quick-paced narrative format that, while jumping between events and characters in a way that makes it hard to get an overall picture of anarchism in Argentina at the time, certainly does bring to the fore the romanticism and adventurism of the expropriators of the title. Much of the attention is given over to the group that converged around the *La Protesta* anarchist newspaper and the anarcho-communist minority splinter group that broke off from the Argentine Regional Workers' Federation (FORA) in 1915. The key figures who appear in the book include the Russian Boris Wladimirovich, the Italians Miguel Roscigna and Severino Di Giovanni, and Buenaventura Durruti. Durruti, of course, went on to play an important role in the anarchist revolution in Spain in the 1930s, but a decade earlier spent time in Argentina.

While much of the book recounts the daring exploits of the anarchist expropriators, it is also laced with farce. Two of the raids Durruti led in Argentina were poorly planned and resulted in negligible rewards for the robbers. As the names listed above may suggest, anarchism in Argentina during this period was a highly international affair, and Bayer's book singles out only a single Argentine-born expropriator as worthy of mention. The internationalism of the anarchists included in the narrative allows Bayer to turn to events elsewhere and he provides an account of the conviction and execution of Sacco and Vanzetti and the response from Argentine anarchists that came in the form of a series of 'terrorist' attacks.

Support for anarchist comrades included jailbreaks as well as robberies and attacks on high officials. Bayer tells the remarkable story of one such jailbreak that involved a professionally-dug tunnel, large enough for a person to walk through without much difficulty, which went under the nearby prison.

Bayer's book, however, is not limited to tales of derring-do on the part of Argentina's radical anarchist movement. He is also careful to detail the repression and counter-attacks targeted not only at the expropriators but at anarchists in general in Argentina in the 1920s and 1930s. Ultimately, the author is pessimistic about the possibility of success of the kinds of actions included in the book and he closes with the following: 'We have just recounted the sordid and epic tale of men who opted for a difficult and heroic solitary path and followed it to its bitter end, to its abrupt and final conclusion. History was not on their side because the solutions for which society seeks can never be reached by such lonely by-ways' (p134).

Thomas Swann, Loughborough University

Janet Biehl, *Ecology or Catastrophe: The Life of Murray Bookchin*

Oxford: Oxford University Press, 2015; 336pp; ISBN 9780199342488

In recent years, there has been a resurgence of interest in the work of leftist political philosopher Murray Bookchin. Given these events, now seems like a perfect time for the release of a biography about this thinker who dedicated his life to bringing about a coherent vision of a truly democratic and ecological society. Such a book might help those interested in radical and coherent social change learn about Bookchin's personal life, his development as a thinker, and the interplay between his pioneering ideas and the environments in which they flourished. Last year, Janet Biehl released *Ecology or Catastrophe: the Life of Murray Bookchin*, a biographical sketch of Bookchin, her live-in partner of eighteen years. While Biehl accomplishes some of these goals, upon reading the book we found that it also contains troublesome omissions and misrepresentations of Bookchin's personal life and political work. As students of Bookchin's close friends and collaborators we could see that these were frequently errors of omission, and thus difficult for the average reader to detect. Our concern was shared by a number of Bookchin scholars, friends, students, and family, spurring additional research and our critical re-examination of the biography.

In *Ecology or Catastrophe* Biehl narrates Bookchin's personal and political development in thirteen chronological and thematic chapters. Setting the stage through extensive research about 1930s-1950s-era politics and leftism, Biehl follows his upbringing in the depression-era Bronx through the New Left, the Anti-

Nuclear Movement, the Green Movement, and his critical engagement with most of the major movements on the Left.

For the first sixty-five years of this story, Biehl must rely on others for information. Yet rather than drawing on her interviews and accounts from those close to Bookchin at the time, Biehl relies heavily on personal recollection of Bookchin's beliefs and motivations. This approach erases from the narrative key figures behind some of Bookchin's major activist projects.

A first example of this kind of omission regards the Anarchos group (1966-1971), the publishing collective and affinity group based in New York City led by Bookchin and his then-wife Bea Bookchin. It was during this period, surrounded by the revolutionary spirit of the New Left, urban uprisings, and 1960s radical cultural experiments, that Bookchin published some of his most salient work about ecology, post-scarcity anarchism, Marxism, and alternative forms of political organisation. Within the electric atmosphere of the late-1960s Lower East Side, the Anarchos group played an important historical role by articulating the powerful affinity between ecological and anarchist thought.[1] Yet despite the importance of this political group, virtually nothing is said in Biehl's book about its members, contributions, and position.

The omission of the Anarchos group and other events ties closely to the conspicuous absence of Bea Bookchin, who was personally and politically close to Murray Bookchin for six decades. Murray Bookchin was married to Bea Bookchin from 1952 until 1963, yet continued to live with her as a close friend, confidant, and housemate for a total of thirty-five years. While any biographer must make decisions about what things to leave out, it is difficult to view Biehl's account of Bookchin's life as credible when such a key individual is entirely absent from the book. For instance, Bea was a central figure in the Burlington Greens during the group's entire duration from 1981-1991. She ran twice for city council as a Green candidate, and spearheaded the Green opposition to a Burlington waterfront development. Despite this, Biehl's sole mention of Bea in this period is a passing reference to the words 'Bea for Burlington' in a campaign poster she claims Bookchin disliked (p262).

Similar problems are extant in regard to most of Bookchin's close comrades and intellectual collaborators, especially women. Biehl's erasure of virtually all of the other women who participated in Bookchin's political milieu paints Biehl as the sole female protagonist in Bookchin's life, and, whether intentionally or not, is a distortion of those women's sensibility and intellectual reach.

Lastly, Biehl's biography becomes problematic in her portrayal of Bookchin himself. In the book's final chapter, which takes place during the last five years of his life, a wealth of odd and inappropriate personal anecdotes takes over the narrative. She seems to oscillate from adoration and awe of Bookchin, to degradation and belittlement. Contrary to Biehl's depiction, Bookchin was not the despondent and confused man present at various junctures in this book. As a philosophical idealist, Bookchin often chided those around him out of depressive thoughts, declaring political cynicism and despair as an admission of defeat to an irrational society.

We appreciate that the depiction of a powerful, complex and dynamic thinker is a challenging endeavour – particularly for an author so intimately related to her subject. We can understand, even though Biehl eventually departed from his political philosophy (p306), why she might want to share her intimate knowledge about Bookchin's life, and offer him some of the long overdue credit he deserves. Yet, by diminishing people crucial to Bookchin's life, Biehl has deprived her readers of an accurate understanding of Bookchin's political background, sensibility, and influences. No biography is ever complete or objective, yet a full and accurate account of this fascinating, complex, and important figure remains to be told.

Eleanor Finley, University of Massachusetts Amherst, PhD student, Institute for Social Ecology, and Dr Federico Venturini, Independent Researcher and Activist, Transnational Institute for Social Ecology

NOTES

1. Andrew Cornell, *Oppose and Propose!: Lessons from Movement for a New Society*, (Oakland: AK Press, 2011), p13.

Penny Rimbaud, *The Last of the Hippies. An hysterical romance*

Oakland: PM Press, 2015; 128pp; ISBN 9781629631035

In *The Last of the Hippies*, Penny Rimbaud celebrates the life of Phil 'Wally' Hope, and rails against his murder at the hands of the state in 1975. In so doing, he conveys some of the anarchist/pacifist philosophy which fed into Crass, and subsequently much of the rest of the anarcho-punk sub-genre. This is actually a fourth publication of *The Last of the Hippies*. It was originally included with

Crass's *Christ, The Album* in 1982, and much of the material was also covered in Rimbaud's autobiography, *Shibboleth: My revolting life* (AK Press, 1998). Active Distribution produced a paperback version of *The Last of the Hippies* in 2009, and this 2015 PM Press edition is almost identical to that, but comes with a slick new cover and a considerable price-hike – up from Active Distro's £1 (yes, *one* pound) to $12! The hurried re-issue may be explained by PM Press's *arguably* wider reach in the US, but the price disparity is stark, and in fact the Active Distribution edition is still in print (and, incidentally, in stock at www.activedistribution.org/shop).

The main body of the text provides a snapshot of Rimbaud, Crass, and the anarcho-punk scene at a particular juncture, immediately after the Falklands War in 1982, with the pacifist emphasis that might be expected therein. However, the 'peace punk' mentality is in sharp contrast to Rimbaud's introduction, written in 2008, which flatly eschews pacifism. Rimbaud writes: 'Crass caught me at a time when pacifism seemed to be the best way forward. Just at the moment, in 2008, I've swung heavily in the opposite direction' (p9). This may come as a surprise to anyone familiar with Crass's lyrics and slogans, but it is always interesting to be able to trace the trajectory of an individual's political positions, and the 'anarchism' of Crass was always a wee bit half-baked, as Rimbaud freely admits.

Rimbaud also jettisons his erstwhile enthusiasm for rock'n'roll's revolutionary potential, an element of *The Last of the Hippies* that now 'greatly embarrasses' him (p12). This change of position has not diminished Rimbaud's cutting wit, however. Bulldozing his way through the revered grandfathers of punk, he writes: 'let's face it, the Pistols were no more than the Spice Girls of their day, glitzy, cheap and, dare I say it, downright crass. The Clash came in at a close second as ABBA with attitude' (p12). And this is really what Crass, and anarcho-punk in general, were best at – firing punk's critique of the music industry back at punk itself, while committing themselves to build something more meaningful than the hypocrisy of the corporate sell-outs.

Also in the introduction, Rimbaud writes that he 'loathe[s] the fad for retro-punk' (p4), but within two years of writing this, Crass succumbed to the retro-punk cash cow with the announcement of Crass vocalist Steve Ignorant's farcical 'Last Supper' and 'Feeding of the 5000' tours (to which Rimbaud gave his blessing), and the subsequent re-issuing of Crass's back-catalogue as 'The Crassical Collection'. And in 2012 it was with bitter irony that Crass themselves were touted as sell-outs for their instrumental role (via Southern Records) in crippling the anarcho-punk.net peer-to-peer music sharing website.

Crass's reputation may have been sullied by the controversies of recent years, but *The Last of the Hippies* stands as a testament to a former integrity, and remains valuable as such.

Jim Donaghey, Just Books (radical literature and more – www.belfastsolidarity.org)

Jeremy Brecher, *Strike!* (Revised, Expanded and Updated Edition)
Oakland: PM Press, 2014; 480pp; ISBN 9781604864281

The most recent edition of *Strike!*, originally published in 1971, makes a major contribution to our understanding of North American labour history. Brecher offers an inspirational, yet sobering, examination of workers' struggles against the exploitative forces of capitalism, and in the process demonstrates how they sought to gain control over their lives.

The first six chapters vividly describe some of labour's epic struggles that illustrate the book's core themes: the enduring tradition of resistance to corporate authority; the creative tactics adopted by workers; and the power of solidarity, transcending race, ethnicity and gender. Starting with the Great Upheaval of 1877, when working class communities rose up against railway tycoons and shook the ruling order, through the sit down strikes in the rubber and automobile industries, which signalled the emergence of the Congress of Industrial Organisations and the legitimisation of workers' collective bargaining rights, *Strike!* tells a story of labour militancy and insurgency.

In the process the author provides a salutary correction to the conventional view that workers in the US lacked class consciousness. In the Pullman Boycott (1894) skilled workers from craft unions were willing to support the producers of railway sleeping cars even in the face of federal court injunctions. During the Great Steel Strike (1919) Eastern European immigrant workers were prepared to stand side-by-side with their more skilled American-born cohorts in an attempt to gain union recognition.

However, Brecher's account of these strikes reminds the reader that many ended in defeat. This was especially true during the 1980s and 1990s when US companies waged a 'one-sided class war', which despite the deployment of new tactics, including corporate campaigns that targeted companies' creditors and community-labour coalitions, resulted in workers' and unions' concessions on wages and benefits in core industries such as automobile manufacturing, steel making, and meatpacking. Concomitantly, union density plummeted from twenty-seven per cent in 1979 to fifteen per cent in 1996, and the accumulative toll of lockouts and defeated strikes sapped workers' militancy as the number of strikes dropped from over 200 per year to under fifty over the same period.

Yet to the author's credit he does not settle for a descriptive narrative of workers' resistance. In a chapter entitled 'The Significance of Mass Strikes' he identifies and analyses the salient characteristics of these upheavals. He punctures the conventional wisdom that the US was a 'class conflict free society' and that workers acquiesced in their situation. Drawing on Rosa Luxemburg, Brecher sees the mass strike as a 'revolutionary process' whereby the participants 'contest the power of existing authorities' and thereby allow for the 'transformation' of workers from 'passive and isolated individuals to a collective of self-directing co-operators operating on their own behalf' (p299). Although he recognises that most of the strikes he discusses aimed to defend or gain improvements in the terms and conditions of employment, Brecher nevertheless stresses their wider implications for the development of a transformative social movement.

Yet this strength of *Strike!* simultaneously reveals a shortcoming. His study serves as a welcome alternative to the institutionalist school of labour history, for it adopts a bottom up approach to organised labour activity, with an emphasis on informal forms of organisation and networking which fostered effective communication and mobilisation. However, it thereby does not do justice to social movement theories which underscore the role of institutions in providing the resources for effective collective action.

This criticism notwithstanding, *Strike!* is an impressive work which deserves the widest readership by scholars and activists alike, not only for its rich detailed accounts of workers' struggles but as a reminder that for 150 years Americans declared, 'another world is possible'.

Ron Mendel, Northampton University

Gavin Bowd, *The Last Communard. Adrien Lejeune, the Unexpected Life of a Revolutionary*

London and New York: Verso, 2016; 182pp; ISBN 9781784782856

The Commune of Paris is a capital event in French history, the importance and impact of which is still being debated – its symbolic value cannot be underestimated. It turns out, as Gavin Bowd shows us in this book (an English translation of a study published originally by L'Harmattan in 2007), that the mythology surrounding the events of 1871 and the consequences they had in the development of French history and politics throughout the twentieth century, echoed much further than could be anticipated. As far away, actually, as Siberia, where Adrien Lejeune, the last survivor of the Commune, died in 1942 in exile during World War Two at ninety-five years of age, while the German armies were occupying his native Paris and getting close to his second home Moscow, from which he was evacuated together with other elderly exiled revolutionaries who had sought refuge in the USSR.

This book is not properly speaking a biography. It is a voyage of discovery through the actual life of Lejeune – or at least what can be known of it, reconstructed through the often contradictory accounts he gave of himself, and those found in the French and Soviet press – and, more importantly, his image. It remains to be seen whether Lejeune was in fact the heroic fighter for the rights of the people that he was eventually transformed into by state and party propaganda, but Bowd paints the portrait of a restless young man who, like many others in similar situations during those difficult times, found himself swept up in events much bigger than he could have anticipated. That he did fight for the Commune and against the Versaillais is undoubted, but his fame rests much more on the twist of fate that made him the last living protagonist of that chaotic and generous attempt at social revolution.

Much of the book deals with the uses of the history of the Commune in Russian and French communist propaganda, where the short-lived self-government set up by the Parisian people, besieged by both the Prussian enemy and the bourgeois Republican army, was presented as the ancestor of the Russian revolution and as a shining example to be followed for the Western European proletariat. In the midst of all that, from internal *Parti communiste français* politicking to the slow-moving Russian bureaucracy, busy with much weightier and more urgent items, Lejeune, in his last years, appears like a slightly pathetic figure, waiting for the care packages that could occasionally be sent to him from home – chocolate, a bottle of wine – seldom able to communicate with other French-speaking exiles or with devoted but overworked polyglot Russian caretakers. Bowd's careful and extensively documented work reconstructs both the actual life and the public image of this involuntary hero, up until the return of his body to Paris, amongst much fanfare, and its interment at the Père Lachaise cemetery, near the famous Mur des Fédérés. This is a thought-provoking and well-constructed book which will appeal to all students of ideology and of the French history of the time. It is also just a good read, an interesting story told with much human sympathy – and that's not an achievement to be scoffed at.

Vittorio Frigerio, Dalhousie University

A.W. Zurbrugg (ed.), *Bakunin. Selected Texts 1868-1875*, translated by A.W. Zurbrugg

London: The Merlin Press, 2016; 300pp; ISBN 9780850367225

What is the significance of translating fragmentary additions to the corpus of a thinker whose work is already acknowledged to be fragmentary, not least by the man himself? Bakunin's writing, which was more united with his political activism than was true of any other nineteenth-century thinker, Marx included, was attacked from the beginning as being disjointed and hurried. Some of the attacks were probably justified in Russia, Bakunin's home country, in the late 1830s, because Bakunin had recently abandoned his noble origins, with the stable publishing platform they would surely have provided. But the 1830s was also the time when Bakunin, lurking in Moscow's reading rooms and drinking halls, developed a *speculative* philosophical orientation. This speculative approach, informed and sustained by Bakunin's familiarity with Hegel, made Bakunin more confident to experience the content and form of his writing differently than if he had worked within the Enlightenment tradition. A decision for interpreters of Bakunin to make is whether to follow Bakunin to an epistemology that, as Nietzsche later said, is 'beyond good and evil', or whether to insist that Bakunin be read conventionally, to see his inability to produce coherent and lucid theoretical work as a sign of his limited faculties.[1] Bakunin's most forceful attempt to address, or explain the fragmentary nature of his writing and his itinerant political lifestyle came in 1882: 'My life itself is a fragment', he acknowledged without any pretension in *God and the State*.[2] The issue that is provoked through editorial and translation work, such as Zurbrugg has done on Bakunin, therefore, is not whether new additions to Bakunin's published corpus will facilitate re-appraisals of Bakunin's significance, but whether Bakunin has ever really been read appropriately in the first place. As well as providing a glossary of key terms, and selecting quotations from Bakunin's texts in an attempt to present the fragmentary writings contained in this volume in their appropriate context, Zurbrugg does address the methodological questions that Bakunin's authorial ineptness and incoherence have provoked, if only hinting at them.

Bakunin used Hegel in three distinct, separable ways as Bakunin's thought ran and developed: firstly, to eschew the ideals of the Enlightenment as a rebellious teenager in the first throes of serious intellectual work; secondly, as a negative point of departure towards socialism; and thirdly, as a faded memory which barely touched his own anarchist edifice. In my opinion, the purview covered by

Zurbrugg's anthology catches Bakunin at what was his most interesting time: his (failed) struggle to identify with the trajectory of the International Working Men's Association led by Marx, culminating in his resignation. In 1868, the first year covered by Zurbrugg's omnibus, Marx and Bakunin constituted something of a team countering Pierre-Joseph Proudhon's influence on the 'League of Peace and Freedom', an alternative to the IWMA that had international pacifism as its core aspiration. By the time of the end of The Hague Congress, held from the 2-7 September 1872, Bakunin's dissatisfaction with Marx's socialism culminated in Bakunin exiting the IWMA along with his friend, the Swiss James Guillaume. In *Statism and Anarchy* (1873), Bakunin pitched his most excoriating criticisms of Marx and Marx's statism. 'Both the theory of the state and the theory of so-called revolutionary dictatorship', Bakunin argued:

> are based on [a] fiction of pseudo-popular representation – which in actual fact means the government of the masses by an insignificant handful of privileged individuals, elected (or not even elected) by mobs of people rounded up for voting and never knowing what or whom they are voting for – on this imaginary and abstract expression of the imaginary thought and will of all the people, of which the real, living people do not have the faintest idea.[3]

Bakunin was also battling, in the years covered by Zurbrugg's omnibus, with his trenchant commitments to the cause of pan-Slavism. Those commitments had been in interface with his internationalist and universalist goal of the overthrow of the autocratic order for decades – for example from 1848 on, when he released his *Appeal to the Slavs*, a pamphlet that encouraged Slav revolutionaries to unite with Hungarians, Italians and Germans to overrun the three hallowed European autocracies: the Russian Empire, the Austro-Hungarian Empire, and the Kingdom of Prussia. But Bakunin's ill-feelings with Marx were the major theme of the years covered by Zurbrugg's omnibus, with Bakunin having written *Recollections on Marx and Engels* between 1869 and 1871. In this anti-Marxist vein, Zurbrugg presents a previously untranslated pamphlet, 'Prospects for Socialism: September 1870', written when Bakunin was already beginning to have doubts, as well as a more fundamentally derogatory pamphlet, 'Writings against Marx: November-December 1872'. In the latter, Bakunin seems very angry at his realisation, which arrived quite suddenly in the early-1870s, that 'Mr Engels and Mr Marx would like to submit [the great masses] to the paternal regime of a *very strong government*' (p229). 'Mr Marx has shown himself', Bakunin explains, 'firstly to be a very bad and very untruthful historian, and secondly not an international socialist revolutionary but rather an ardent patriot of the greater Bismarckian nation' (pp223-4).

'Bakunin had defects', Zurbrugg willingly concedes, 'he was not a disciplined writer' (p26). 'James Guillaume once noted, "As an author he had no vanity [amour-propre] he said of himself that "he completely lacked the talent of an architect in literature" and that when he "built his house" he needed a friend "to put in the doors and windows".[4] 'His writings often contains [sic] digressions, turning from one subject to another, but, as Paul Avrich notes, despite their fragmentary nature, his writing abounds in "flashes of insight".[5] Zurbrugg's familiarity with the questions that Bakunin's authorial style provokes is evident in the way Zurbrugg contextualises each piece. Zurbrugg's curatorial skills and an eclectic and interesting range of fragments are what make this volume as a whole easy to recommend to the casual or specialist reader.

Sebastian Averill, Loughborough University

NOTES

1. Friedrich Nietzsche, *Nietzsche: Beyond Good and Evil: Prelude to a Philosophy of the Future*, Rolf-Peter Horstmann (ed.), Judith Norman (trans.), (New York, NY, and Cambridge: Cambridge University Press, 2002), p60.
2. Mikhail Bakunin, *God and the State*, Paul Avrich (ed.), (Mineola, NY: Dover Publications, 1970) p6.
3. Mikhail Bakunin, M., *Statism and Anarchy*, Marshall S. Shatz (trans.), (Cambridge: Cambridge University Press, 1990), pp136-7.
4. Letter to Herzen, 28 October 1869, quoted in 'Les Ours de Berne et l'Ours de Saint Pétersbourg', (Neuchâtel: G. Guillaume Fils, 1870), re-published in Mikhail Bakunin, *Oeuvres* 2, p8.
5. Paul Avrich, *Anarchist Portraits*, (Princeton: Princeton University Press, 1988), p6.

Jason Garner, *Goals and Means: Anarchism, Syndicalism, and Internationalism in the Origins of the Federación Anarquista Ibérica*

Edinburgh: AK Press, 2016; 384pp; ISBN 9781849352253

For understandable reasons, many studies of Spanish anarchism encompass the period from the foundation of the Second Republic to the end of the Spanish Civil War

(1931-1939), which saw the apogee and tragedy of the movement's principal organisation, the National Confederation of Labour (CNT). This new book, which traces the turbulent trajectory of the CNT and the place of anarchism within it in the decades before the Second Republic, thus provides a great service to those in the Anglophone world interested in the earlier history of the Spanish anarchist movement.

Garner focuses on the attempts of activists within the CNT to marry the goal of libertarian communism to the means of industrial syndicalism. This was a far from simple task, and the book highlights the many controversies that complicated the relationship between the organisation's anarchist and syndicalist wings. The author argues that it was only through an effective unity of both that the movement in Spain could avoid succumbing to either gradualist reformism or impotent purism. Anarcho-syndicalism was the term that came to express this synthesis, but its practical implementation was impeded by bitter doctrinal disputes. For the 'purist' anarchists, the gradualism of the syndicalists had the whiff of Marxism and political ambition, while for the syndicalists, the overt association of the union organisation with any one ideology would fatally undermine its attractiveness to the working class. The Iberian Anarchist Federation (FAI), founded in 1927, attempted to address this problem. Its members were expected to devote themselves selflessly to union activity but would also seek to prevent its quotidian tasks from becoming the be-all and end-all of the CNT. While the FAI would go on to play an important role in the anarchist movement during the Second Republic, it could not overcome the mutual distrust between the more organisationally-focused and more ideologically-focused tendencies.

Garner's detailed tracking of these disputes during the turbulent years of street violence, dictatorship and exile makes this monograph a likely point of reference for any future English-language study of twentieth-century Spanish anarchism. However, its focus on the politics of the movement, while illuminating, presents the danger of privileging the outlook and practice of key activists and organisations over circumstantial factors. When this is combined with a polemical style, the result is unsatisfying, and there are occasions when this combination makes Garner's interpretations unconvincing, particularly when discussing the failure of Bolshevism to establish itself within the CNT and the parlous state of anarchism in France in the 1920s.

The 'internationalism' of the book's subtitle refers to organisational contacts and ideological affinities. Garner shows how Spanish activists were attentive to international debates and in contact with foreign militants and organisations, emphasising the influence of Malatesta on the movement's adherents, and the role of Portuguese activists in the formation of the FAI. In spite of this cosmopolitanism, however, when many Spanish activists found themselves exiled in France in the 1920s, Garner affirms that the flawed strategic perspectives and consequent irrelevance of the miniscule French movement meant that its activists had 'nothing to teach' their Spanish counterparts. Nevertheless, this milieu would later provide several of the more cogent critiques of the CNT's activity during the civil war. The Spanish anarchists, in spite of their humbling achievements and organisational and ideological innovations, were, like their French counterparts, unable to escape the bitter consequences of defeat. Garner's book is a welcome reminder that they still have much to teach us.

Danny Evans

Osvaldo Bayer, *Rebellion in Patagonia*, translated by Paul Sharkey and Joshua Neuhouser

Chico, Oakland, Edinburgh, Baltimore: AK Press, 2016; 525pp; ISBN 9781849352215

It is indeed daunting to say something new or meaningful of a book as widely read, commented and even filmed as Bayer's *Rebellion in Patagonia*. The English translation of this classic of anarchist literature can hardly be more timely or welcome in these present times of duress. The degree of detail, the vivacity of the narration, and the passion it conveys made it an instant, but heavily contested, success.

Since the aftermath of the Wars of Independence at the beginning of the nineteenth century, local communities in Patagonia had faced exploitation at the hands of foreign capitalists, racial discrimination, class war, and ethnic cleansing. The Argentine army had been used to massacre the local Mapuche population in the successive Campaña del Desierto ('Desert campaign') led by General Juan Manuel Rosas in 1833 and 1834, and the Conquest of the Desert in the 1870s. Military counter-insurgency had been used to 'protect' the local white population and the interests of over-powerful businessmen and landowners, as well as to curb Mapuche rides, 'malones', which mostly originated in the unlawful eviction and the subsequent occupation of their lands.

Since the late-nineteenth century, this contentious and inhospitable land hosted a large number of exiled French, German, Italian, Russian, and Spanish anarchists and socialists. Bayer's book (2001), initially published in a longer, four-volume work entitled *The Avengers of Patagonia* (1972-1978), accounts for the hardships the working classes went through and their organisational struggles (and successes too). It reconstructs the conflicts and resistance campaigns led by local and exiled peasants and skilled workers, mobilised against the harrowing conditions imposed by unscrupulous exploiters. The extraordinary accumulation of wealth which concentrated in the hands of a sizeable group of rich families in the region, originating in sheer exploitation of the local labour force as well as in privileged access to international trade markets, back lashed in the late-1910s.

Workers' living and working conditions had further worsened with the arrival, in 1916, of the alleged 'reformist' government headed by Hipólito Yrigoyen, the leader of the Radical Civic Union. The reduction of salaries and the sustained repression of the activities carried out by the unions and affinity groups linked to the FOA (Argentine Workers Federation), the UGT (General Union of Workers), and the FORA (Argentine Regional Workers' Federation) led to open rebellion in 1920. For eighteen months a series of strikes, land collectivisation, kidnaps and shootings would show the lengths to which these oppressed farmers were willing to go to defend their dignity.

Bayer's take on the revolutionary wave between 1920 and 1922 in Patagonia is painstakingly documented. He not only draws on bosses' and workers' publications, correspondence and memoirs, and official materials held in the military and police archives, but also interviews some survivors and eyewitnesses. The crucial role of women, gauchos and non-member external actors in the strikes and the land occupations is highlighted in order to enrich the analysis of a social and political movement which unsuccessfully tried to put a halt to the abuses of a ruthless high bourgeoisie too scared by the events of the 1917 Bolshevik revolution to be bothered to respect basic human rights. The Argentine army was in the 1920s, as in later decades, far too ready to assist them. The death toll was striking with more than 1500 peons executed by soldiers and officers who put their sabres at the service of alleged 'national security' and international capitalist interest. In so doing they wiped out the seeds for further rebellion and opposition against well-connected ruling classes. Let Bayer's work keep the memory of those fighters alive.

Gregorio Alonso, University of Leeds

A.W. Zurbrugg (ed.), *Not Our War. Writings against the First World War*
London: The Merlin Press, 2014; 242pp; ISBN 9780850366143

The centenary of the start of the First World War has spawned quite a number of editorial revisits to that particularly awful page of history. While we have been mostly spared rhetorical excesses, at least at the level at which they were common during the conflict itself, critical views of the war still often shy away from calling that immense, needless butchery the unconscionable crime against humanity that it really was. And when they do, they also often show remarkable discretion when pointing the finger at the true culprits, on all sides. Zurbrugg's anthology of anti-war writings suffers from no such timidity. Divided into four, widely unequal parts, it exhumes declarations and excerpts from dozens and dozens of militants, simple soldiers, journalists, agitators, writers, and all sorts of witnesses to the horrors of the war that was supposed to end all wars.

The first (rather short) section, entitled 'I wept', offers reactions to the breakout of the war by such names as Louis Lecoin, Angelica Balabanoff, John Reed, Emma Goldman and other lesser-known or unknown people. The second, entitled 'Against Militarism', could have been subtitled 'I told you so', considering the number of prescient denunciations of the upcoming massacre it contains, through the voices of activists such as Malatesta, Lenin, Liebknecht, and various anonymous sources. The third, 'Civilization', focuses on the broken promises made to the colonial populations who were made to fight a war which was not their own, only to be ignored or repressed when, at its end, they asked for the equal rights they thought they had earned. Finally, 'Duty? What Duty?' speaks to the questions of patriotism, anti-patriotism and internationalism, the justifications for the war, and the socialists' reactions to them. Amongst the authors cited we note Makhno, Trotsky, Sébastien Faure, Big Bill Haywood and many pamphlets from various workers' groups. Each section is preceded by a concise introduction of a few pages in length, there is also a general introduction to the volume, 'Some final thoughts' at the end, as well as a brief 'Timeline of International and National Events', ending with a useful 'Index of persons, journals and organisations'. The quotes have been garnered from a remarkable number of different original sources, although many have also been found surfing the internet. Each excerpt is followed by a few lines of comment, to offer information on the authors (many of them unknown) or their particular situation and to provide historical context. As the editor notes, some texts appear for the first time in English.

This book is certainly an interesting read, as a testimony of the times and a welcome reminder of the reality of the war and of its consequences – including what it did to the anti-militarist movement, to the various branches of the socialist movement, and to the anarchists, who took a long time to recover from Kropotkin's (and others') adherence to the 'Union sacrée'. Sometimes, the quotes are too short to be truly satisfying on their own, but their accumulative effect is impactful; the surprise of finding the same analysis and the same conclusions coming from actors operating in widely different parts of the 'theatre of operations', to borrow a military term. At a time when nationalism seems again to be resurgent in Europe, the lessons that can be drawn from such an anthology remain valid, and its picture of the inability or unwillingness of socialists of all stripes to put their theories into action is both downright depressing and uncannily current. It is striking to see how cogent critics of militarism could be silenced by the powers that be and ignored or dismissed by a fanaticised general population – with the tragic consequences we know all too well. At times, being obviously right is not enough to be heard, even though, as Rosa Luxemburg exclaims irritably in one of these excerpts: 'Even a poorly informed student of history knows' (p134). Thanks to books such as this, the next time we will be able to say with even more certainty that everybody should have known.

Vittorio Frigerio, Dalhousie University

Eirik Eiglad (ed.), *Social Ecology and Social Change*
Porsgrunn: New Compass Press, 2015; 258pp; ISBN 9788293064343

Social Ecology and Social Change brings together nineteen interesting and informative essays from the 2014 Ecological Challenges conference in Oslo, aiming to demonstrate how social ecology theory connects with real life issues and how it might concretely influence social change towards communalism. The book overviews some of the main concerns of social ecology today, e.g. climate change, rapid urbanisation, transport, environmental conflicts, organised crime, and explains how social ecology addresses global problems such as these. Among the chapters are case studies from the United States, Canada, Brazil, Czech Republic, Italy, Turkey, and Iraq. Social movements around the world are encouraged to increase their awareness of the current ecological crisis, and of potential solutions to it.

Some of the most insightful essays here include Eirik Eiglad's and Dan Chodorkoff's opening essays, which provide a foundational introduction to social ecology theory, followed by Brian Tokar's and Sveinung Legard's fascinating texts, asking what can be done to counter the impact of climate change. While taking different approaches, Tokar and Legard both suggest participatory democracy as a method to challenge climate change.

Mat Little warns that the contradictions of capitalism have come to the fore, and that, contrary to predictions of social ecologists, the system is crumbling. Adam Krause acknowledges that capitalism's collapse seems imminent, but this hasn't stopped the looting of our planet because capitalism as a system 'manages to supply basic needs for enough people [so] only a small minority ever hit the streets' (p89). Apparently, getting organised requires too much effort, as people are busy just trying to make a living – which seems to condemn ordinary people to the status quo.

Marco R. Rossi interestingly discusses the 'civic nature of socialism' instead of its commonly emphasised economic aspect, pointing out that the core issue within leftist theory today is that 'it has not matured beyond the world described by its founders' (p99). John Nightingale, drawing especially on Bookchin, provides an excellent summary of how social ecology conceptualises citizenship and solidarity – though it would have been preferable to see this contribution earlier in the book.

Two interesting essays which raise questions about urban transport, planning, and design are Janet Biehl's 'The American Built Environment as an Ecological Challenge' and Ersilia Verlinghieri's 'Radical Approaches to Transport Planning'. Biehl astutely demonstrates the disastrous effects of the automobile on the environment *and* social relations. In the USA, entire communities and suburban areas were designed to encourage car use, eventually leading to a lack of social interaction, with people confined to the private sphere, only interacting with the rest of the world via technological devices. 'Good urban design' and 'smart growth', Biehl points out, should also focus on how to (re-)strengthen social bonds and community spirit. Ersilia Verlinghieri is critical of the slow rate of progress and lack of radical approaches to urban planning. While acknowledgeing an increasing awareness of sustainable transport (walking and cycling), she criticises city transport planners and academicians in transport studies for focusing on engineering solutions and top-down strategies that ignore public participation.

Arnošt Novák argues that current Czech environmental groups are trying to fix capitalism's broken system in vain, criticising them for abandoning the struggle for social change. Jonathan Korsár attempts to integrate Bookchin's libertarian municipalism with Jeremy Rifkin's concept of the 'zero marginal cost society'. Salvatore Paolo de Rosa and Monica Caggiano discuss communities in Campania, Italy, which have taken action to protect their environment against the illegal and detrimental activities of the mafia.

Metin Güven analyses why Bookchin's 'Third Revolution' has not been achieved and how it might be realised, but the 'Third Revolution' concept would have been better explained earlier in the essay. Toon Bijnens and Johanna L. Rivera contribute to knowledge on ecological activism in Iraq with an informative discussion on awareness and movements there. Cağrı Eryılmaz sheds light on the forums and networks that resulted from the 2014 Gezi Park uprisings in Turkey, but further discussion of online forums' distinctiveness from physical forums, in terms of direct democracy in social ecology, could have better supported some of Eryılmaz's claims.

Federico Venturini's highly valuable contribution examines the reciprocal influence between the practices of urban social movements in Rio de Janeiro and ecology theory. Camilla Hansen provides a detailed yet concise account of participatory democracy from an Arendtian perspective, though her distinction between scientists and citizens with regard to caring for the environment carries the risk of misinterpretation – the political judgement of scientists who think in abstract and neutral language is circumspect in a normative political process which requires us to act as *citizens*. Dimitrios Roussopoulos' closing essay includes an enlightening look at the grassroots movement in Montreal, which has drawn inspiration from communalist ideas.

There is, however, a potential paradox which none of the authors address. Despite their well-founded criticism of Western environmental movements' reformism, it is often the case that these groups are actually the most vocal among environmental groups. Also, public environmental awareness is strongest in countries where capitalism is most entrenched. The book would have benefitted from a discussion on social ecology's response to this perceived contradiction and denial. In addition, readers might recognise capitalism's devastating impact on the environment but also observe that capitalism's rise since the sixteenth century has simultaneously resulted in rapid progress (at least in the West) in technology, science, engineering, medicine, architecture, art, and culture. How does social ecology respond to this? A brief critique raising the perceived benefits of capitalist modernity and their connection to realities such as hierarchy, patriarchy, colonialism, slavery, and exploitation of wage labour would be beneficial.

Overall, the book is easy to read, free of academic jargon, and contains excellent descriptions of social ecology, communalism, participatory democracy, social movements, and the ecological crisis. It is therefore ideal for readers wishing to familiarise themselves with social ecology and its main concerns in contemporary times.

Yagmur Savran, PhD student in Peace Studies, University of Bradford

Cindy Milstein (ed.), *Taking Sides: Revolutionary Solidarity and the Poverty of Liberalism*

Edinburgh: AK Press, 2016; 162pp; ISBN 9781849352321

Taking Sides: Revolutionary Solidarity and the Poverty of Liberalism, a collection of essays put together by Cindy Milstein, is a captivating analysis of selected recent activist politics. The book contains thirteen essays, some of which were initially published as zines, blog pieces, or other formats, and are brought together here to construct a new way of understanding the concepts of solidarity and allyship. Most pieces reflect on organising around indigenous struggles, Black Lives Matter or other black anti-oppression groups, and come from, as Milstein calls them, 'street intellectuals' of the North American context.

The connecting thread of all the essays is the interaction between those involved in these struggles and their 'allies'. Even though the writers sometimes disagree in their discussion of allyship, they all explore the questions of how one can be a good ally, what the possibilities and limits of solidarity are, what roles white people have played in indigenous/black liberation, and what roles they might play in the future.

The cutting critiques in these essays will most likely not come as a surprise to people who have been involved in these or linked struggles. Harsha Walia's 'Decolonise together' talks about white allies being incapacitated by their feelings of guilt and thus unable to join the struggle. 'A Critique of Ally Politics' by M. analyses in depth the concept and practices of allyship as a liberal practice embedded in identity politics – allies, M. claims, need to adopt a certain 'white' identity to acknowledge their privilege (p66). A good ally, the story goes, should support people of colour in their struggles, but since 'people of colour' is not a singular group or identity, which people of colour in particular a good ally should support becomes a fundamental question with a complicated set of answers. To quote: 'The charity and ally models ... are so strongly rooted in the ideas of I and the other that they force people to fit into distinct groups with preordained relationships to one another' (p75). A similar sentiment is expressed in 'Accomplices not Allies', which looks at various ally tropes – white saviours, self-proclaimed allies, parachuters, academics, gatekeepers, navigators and floaters.

Whilst some anarchists may be quick to dismiss these critiques as 'divisive', most of the essays are concerned with creating stronger unions and more possibilities for working together rather than rejecting them. Despite sometimes appearing provocative, the pieces are explicitly framed as prioritising the production of more effective forms of solidarity over criticising previous forms. Walia provides a number of suggestions (p40), as do Neal Shirley and Saralee Stafford (p97). Most essays are full of examples of effective solidarity and successful allying – starting with Michael Staudenmaier's account of Ferguson, Finn Feinberg's surprise at white working-class people joining the Oakland rebellions, and Cindy Milstein's own piece that discusses various occasions when protest was made inclusive, supportive and powerful. The collection is a powerful message to anyone who has ever struggled with navigating how to best show support to oppressed people and is especially relevant for the UK and European context where solidarity politics with migrants, refugees and people of colour is frequently undertaken in such a way that it alienates more people than it attracts. Indeed, the biggest strength of *Taking Sides* is perhaps not its examples and suggestions, but the fact that it brings up a lot of questions that need to be asked – about identity, intersectionality, affinity – and leaves the readers to negotiate the answers in their own relationships.

Solidarity is a difficult concept, not just in terms of theorising, but also in terms of practising it. Solidarity, unlike other feelings that create bonds between people like sympathy or empathy, implies the promise of action or an action itself – or at least this seems to be the implied message of *Taking Sides*. As Indigenous Action Media remark: 'Don't wait around for anyone to proclaim you to be an accomplice: you certainly cannot proclaim it yourself. You just are or you're not' (p96). And since most of the pieces are written by self-identified people of colour, it seems that as an ally the first thing people can do is read carefully and take these points seriously.

Elizabet Vasileva, Loughborough University

Kelly Fritsch, Clare O'Connor and AK Thompson (eds), *Keywords for Radicals: The Contested Vocabulary of Late-Capitalist Struggle*

Edinburgh: AK Press, 2016; 572pp; ISBN 9781849352420

This volume is an adroit variation on the *Keywords* format pioneered by Marxist scholar Raymond Williams in 1976 and expanded in 1983. *Keywords for Radicals* applies Williams' concept in a contemporary setting not only in order to reflect the changing (and, as the subtitle suggests, contested) usage of politically-charged terminology, but also to take a side in that contest. The editors have solicited keyword entries from over fifty contributors, many of them specialists in radical left politics and/or radical activists in their own right.

The radical reader is likely to enjoy, in this latest manifestation of the *Keywords* idea, something of an antidote to the 2005 *New Keywords*,[1] a similar project which, despite the undeniable scholarly merit of its individual entries, was conspicuous in its omission of many radical concepts and terms included in Williams' original. Not least among the casualties of *New Keywords* were entries for Anarchism, Collective, Common, Communism, Labour, Progressive, and Revolution.[2] These and others, the *New Keywords* editors felt, had 'not sustained their importance',[3] or had otherwise lost 'that edge of energy and uncertainty that marks a keyword in public usage'.[4]

Whilst *Keywords for Radicals* does not restore all of these entries to its table of contents, it will no doubt relieve the eponymous radicals to at least see Commons, Labo[u]r and Revolution making a comeback. Two other of Williams' original terms judiciously rescued by *Keywords for Radicals* from the *New Keywords* cull are Hegemony and Violence, neither of which have lost their sting as indispensable terms of critical engagement in the bellicose opening decades of the twenty-first century.

The real thrust of *Keywords for Radicals*, though, lies not in the irredentist recapture of the radical linguistic territory of the original *Keywords*, but in an expedition into radical activity's contemporary vocabulary. The stated aim of the editors in this respect is not only to observationally describe language currently used in the radical milieu (though this is certainly accomplished along the way); they also consider the project to have additional potential as an aid to critical intervention, expediting the lexicon's '"brittle" degeneration so that a new reality and a new understanding might emerge' (p18) as a result of unearthed contradictions in the deployment of terms.

The selection of entries, coupled with a novel method of ordering them, admirably lends itself to precisely this kind of critical activity. Certain key themes are given a multi-faceted treatment by the general tendency of the editors to include several related keywords which reinforce or interrogate one another – for instance, the reader can now traverse from Hegemony to related entries for Authority, Leadership, Sovereignty, etc., or from Violence to Domination, Revolution, War, etc. – and additionally, the interrelationships of such word clusters are visually diagrammed as an overarching networked structure at the start of the book. The nonlinear pattern of each entry's relationship to its peers is explorable by reference to this master diagram, in combination with smaller diagrams throughout the book which highlight the localised connections associated with each entry.

One corollary of this editorial focus on clusters of related keywords is that overall breadth of topic coverage is affected – gone, for instance, are many of the conceptual outliers on the *New Keywords* smorgasbord: Celebrity, Copy, Fashion, Fetish, etc. – although whether this abandonment of generalism should be considered detrimental to the project is likely to depend heavily on the political priorities of the reader. This narrower focus on the vocabulary of the radical left is congruent, however, with the programme of critical linguistic intervention envisioned by the editors in their introduction, in that the fine-grained hunt for 'brittleness' and contradiction is probably much better served by the examination of closely related terms than by a more scattered catalogue of samples drawn from culture and society in their entirety.

The fact that the book differentiates itself from its predecessors by an explicit, partisan titular declaration – *for* radicals – is also worthy of critical reflection in terms of how it might affect its reception and popular appeal. Does *Keywords for Radicals* preach to the choir, courting only an existing radical constituency, however defined? Or can it be *for radicals* in a more ambitious sense, *for* the creation of new radicals? Can it *radicalise*?

In this regard, it actually fares rather well. To begin with, the editors are cognisant of the limited audience of predecessor *Keywords* projects; they are keen to avoid the 'overly academic reception' (p11) with which *Keywords* and *New Keywords* were reportedly met, a consideration which bodes well for the potential public appeal of this volume. To this end, and to the credit of the contributors, the individual entries tend to avoid academic obscurantism, though without sacrificing anything in the way of thorough citation and quality of research.

As to the *for radicals* constraint, it is precisely the overall accessibility of both the format and the actual content of this book that is most suggestive of its capacity to aid in the general promotion of radical ideas. One could easily imagine the volume – eye-catchingly bound and with its engaging visual method of presenting the entries – serving as a sort of introductory gateway into radical politics for the non-radical (or, we might hope, not-yet-radical) general reader, without requiring too much prior fluency either in 'the "insider language" of activist subculture' (p11), or the often equally esoteric insider language of the academy.

That said, any academic designing a course in politics and hoping to inject some radical thought into the mix would do well to consider adopting some of these entries as readings, especially since many of them lead invitingly from condensed, digestible coverage of the idea at hand towards more in-depth referencing of external literature.

James McIntyre, Loughborough University

NOTES

1. Tony Bennett, Lawrence Grossberg, and Meaghan Morris (eds), *New Keywords: A Revised Vocabulary of Culture and Society*, (Blackwell Publishing, Oxford 2005).
2. Some clarification is worthwhile concerning Revolution. Though it was deleted as a stand-alone entry in *New Keywords*, it at least managed to cameo under a consolidated Reform and Revolution heading, where it was cast by contributor Barry Hindess as one side of an 'old debate [...] [which] has largely disappeared from political discourse' (in Bennett et al., op. cit., p304). In delightful contrast, *Keywords for Radicals* contributor Thomas Nail's Revolution entry – sans 'Reform' and perhaps all the better for it – proclaims that '[t]oday we are witnessing the return of Revolution' (p375).
3. Bennett et al., op. cit., xviii.
4. Ibid., xxii-xxiii.

Chris Dixon, *Another Politics: Talking across Today's Transformative Movements*

Oakland: University of California Press, 2014; 363pp; ISBN 9780520279025

Chris Dixon is an anti-authoritarian organiser, and a researcher who has been investigating the latest thinking about goals, strategy, methods and organisation among young, anarchist-inspired activists and organisers in Canada and the US. This insightful book is the result – a worthy read for anyone interested in anarchist theory and practice.

Dixon interviewed dozens of activists, with a few restrictions and emphases. He contacted only those younger than thirty-five years old, seeking views from those involved in current struggles. He made sure his sample included more women than men, and overrepresented ethnic minorities. In this way he counteracted the usual bias towards older white males.

Some of his interviewees thought of themselves as anarchists – most, though, did not, but were inspired by similar ideals. Dixon refers to the 'anti-authoritarian current', which encompasses a variety of perspectives, broadly aligned with anarchist thinking, but he acknowledges that this current is neither large nor highly influential. He interviewed organisers in several large cities, but even there the numbers of activists are comparatively few, and outside the cities the current is even less present. Despite its limited numbers, the current is quite influential in a variety of social movements and struggles. Furthermore, it is developing an approach to social change efforts that, if taken up more widely, has the potential for laying the basis for revolutionary change.

Another Politics is told from Dixon's point of view, in both an individual and collective voice. He is quite willing to present his personal views, but much of the book is told through the words of his interviewees. In part, Dixon imposes his own sense of order to the exposition, while in part it emerges from the priorities and perspectives of those he interviewed. Because of this collective dimension, Dixon often and legitimately refers to 'we'; he is part of the movement. He does not speak for it, but through his research he can offer movement-oriented perspectives.

Dixon tackles topics that are among the most difficult facing anti-authoritarians, in particular strategy and organising. Strategy has long been a weak area for social movements. Many groups focus on campaigns, and are reactive; there is a racist incident, a police beating or the threat of a new law or war, and activists mobilise. This is worthwhile but it means long-term perspectives are submerged and that activism is driven by contingencies and by government and media priorities. It is hard for groups to adhere to efforts moving toward long-term visions without short-term actions and occasional victories to maintain morale. Dixon sees some hope in overcoming this challenge with what he calls a strategic framework.

For strategic purposes, prefigurative politics – behaving according to a vision of a future society – ideally involves a combination of a focus on the here-and-now and a connection to the ultimate goal. Dixon quotes many activists on the need to become engaged with messy current politics, because being purist (setting up a model commune, for example) will have little impact on dominant power systems. On the other hand, focusing on current politics holds the risk of becoming trapped within a reformist dynamic. For example, campaigners need to figure out their relationship with elections. Totally abstaining from electoral politics is a purist option; conventional campaigning for candidates is reformist. Somewhere between is selective engagement while promoting alternatives to electoral systems.

Dixon canvasses a range of issues, including ones that have plagued anarchist politics for decades without satisfactory resolution. One such issue is leadership. Many anti-authoritarians are turned off by dominant models of leadership, which assume hierarchical organisations and unhealthy interpersonal behaviours. However, by rejecting conventional leadership, activists may fail to address the need for different forms of leadership, involving role modelling, mentoring, skill sharing and expertise at the service of the cause. Rather than tearing down anyone who takes a leadership role, the challenge is to construct processes that recognise useful roles for leadership within an egalitarian framework and that nurture leadership skills in many individuals.

Another Politics focuses on Canada and the US, with the limitation that the rest of the world becomes a backdrop. By some accounts, the US government is the coordinator of a contemporary world empire. In this context, concentrating on anti-authoritarian politics in the US is both important and inadequate. It is important because opposition within the core of the empire plays a special role. It is inadequate because opposition within the core should take into account forms and methods of opposition in the periphery, namely everywhere else in the world. Through their campaigns (especially on topics such as militarism and international trade agreements), activists in the US can probe the dynamics of the US state-military-capitalism complex and learn lessons that can be communicated to campaigners elsewhere. Likewise, activists throughout the world can gain insights through their campaigns that can be taken on board by US activists. *Another Politics* is an impressive piece of scholarship, and a vital contribution to the sort of activist dialogue that can build stronger and more strategic movements.

Brian Martin, University of Wollongong

JUST BOOKS IS A RADICAL BOOKSHOP HOUSED AT BELFAST SOLIDARITY CENTRE AND ONLINE.

WE STOCK BOOKS, COMICS, MAGAZINES AND PAMPHLETS TO SUIT ANY RADICAL TASTE:

ANARCHIST, MARXIST, QUEER, FEMINIST, BLACK LIBERATION, ANTI-FASCIST, SYNDICALIST, IRISH HISTORY AND POLITICS, AUTONOMIST, ANIMAL LIBERATION, VEGAN COOKBOOKS AND MORE!

PLUS T-SHIRTS, PATCHES AND PINS.

SHOP ONLINE OR CALL INTO THE SHOP TO SAY HELLO!

WWW.BELFASTSOLIDARITY.ORG

JUSTBOOKSBELFAST@GMAIL.COM +44 28 9543 0203

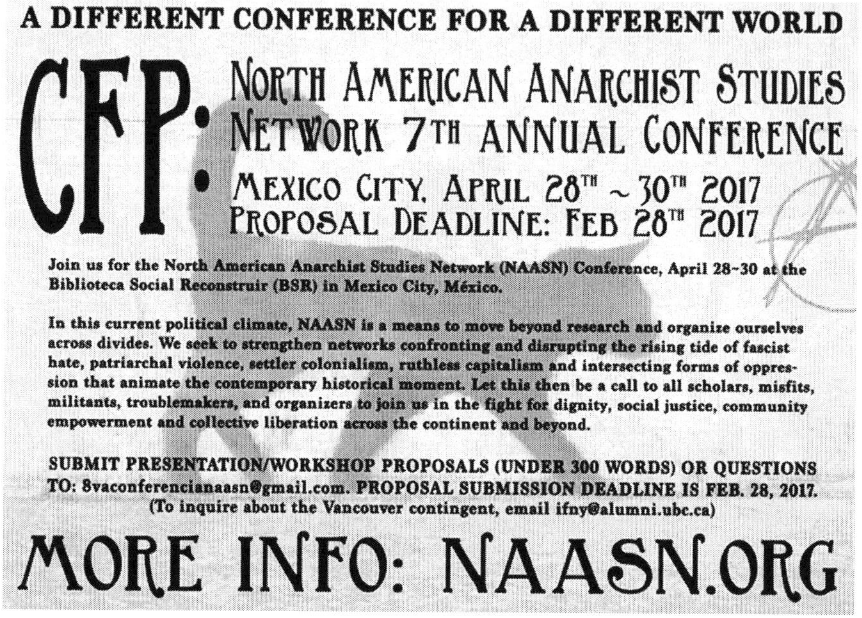

A DIFFERENT CONFERENCE FOR A DIFFERENT WORLD

CFP: North American Anarchist Studies Network 7th Annual Conference

Mexico City, April 28th ~ 30th 2017
Proposal Deadline: Feb 28th 2017

Join us for the North American Anarchist Studies Network (NAASN) Conference, April 28~30 at the Biblioteca Social Reconstruir (BSR) in Mexico City, México.

In this current political climate, NAASN is a means to move beyond research and organize ourselves across divides. We seek to strengthen networks confronting and disrupting the rising tide of fascist hate, patriarchal violence, settler colonialism, ruthless capitalism and intersecting forms of oppression that animate the contemporary historical moment. Let this then be a call to all scholars, misfits, militants, troublemakers, and organizers to join us in the fight for dignity, social justice, community empowerment and collective liberation across the continent and beyond.

SUBMIT PRESENTATION/WORKSHOP PROPOSALS (UNDER 300 WORDS) OR QUESTIONS TO: 8vaconferencianaasn@gmail.com. PROPOSAL SUBMISSION DEADLINE IS FEB. 28, 2017.
(To inquire about the Vancouver contingent, email ifny@alumni.ubc.ca)

MORE INFO: NAASN.ORG

http://naasn.org/sites/default/files/NAASN-new-CFP-english-WEB.jpg